Of Fractured Clocks, Bones and Windshields

A Collection of Poetry

Sheela Sitaram Free

Plain View Press
P. O. 42255
Austin, TX 78704

plainviewpress.net
sb@plainviewpress.net
512-441-2452

Copyright Sheela Sitaram Free, 2009. All rights reserved.
ISBN: 978-0-911051-31-5
Library of Congress Number: 2009921659

Cover art Marc Victory Adams, Semper Fidelis, and Sheela Sitaram Free (concept).

Disclaimer

This book is a work of art with no resemblance to any event, incident, anything or anyone, living or dead.

Acknowledgements and Gratitudes

With deep gratitude and in memoriam to my literary ancestors, my maternal great grandma, Verri Janakiamma, herself a pioneering published writer, my paternal grandma, Alemelu (Alemelamma), my dearest daddy Major Vangala Srinivas Sitaram, my sweet sweet precious little girl Kirti "Kitty", all of who inspired me, motivated me, nourished me with love, tenderness, and a deep belief in my verse and voice.

Tvameva Matah, ch Pitah tvameva
Tvameva Bandhush, ch Sakha tvameva
Tvameva Vidhya, tvameva Dravinam
Tvameva Sarvam, Mama Deva Deva.
                              ~Sanskrit

Thou art my mother, Thou art my father
Thou art my friend, Thou art my comrade
Thou art my knowledge, Thou art my wealth
Thou art my all-in-all
O Gods of gods.
                              ~Prapanna Gita 28.

Don't walk
        in front of me
I may not follow
Don't walk
        behind me
I might not lead
Just walk
        beside me
And be my friend.
                              ~Camus.

Thanks to my Thatthayya, Ammamma, Mummy, and Akka. They know, and to my brother, Vangala Srinivas, my steady rock. He knows.

Thanks to Mrs. Shroff who throughout high school showed me how to stroke and tease the beauty out of words. She knows. To Mrs. Felix and Doveton Corrie Girls High School who pushed me to my fullest potential. They know.

Thanks to Dr. Naomi Lebowitz who over the very many years has been a mentor, friend, and everything in between par excellence. She knows.

Thanks to Myrtle (and her family) for always being there. She knows.

Thanks to Yvette Lee for her unwitting constant inspiration, unwavering support, friendship, and love. She is the catalyst. She knows.

Thanks to the unconscious quiet inspiration of my dear friend and colleague Joel Lamore who always keeps the poetry flame on the front burner. He knows.

Thanks to Gayle Brandeis, who, literally out of the blue, encouraged, supported, guided, and pointed me in the right direction with the kindest of words. She knows.

Thanks to San Bernardino, CA for freeing me up in verse.

Thanks to Susan Bright and her wonderful team at Plain View Press for not only believing in and supporting my voice but also for sharing it with the world.

Thanks to Marc Victory Adams without whom the cover design would not have been possible. His enthusiastic embrace of the project infuses the work with joy.

Contents

San Bernardino Passion	5
San Bernardino Blues	6
Uvulaic Rhapsody	10
And Then the Mountain Dies	11
The Arsonist: Halloween Masquerade	12
I Burn You Burn We All Burn Together	13
CA Witches Brew	16
Maria Oh Maria	18
Shower Stall Swan Song	19
Aqua American	20
Cabo Cabo	21
Loins On the Line	22
Hey Emma, Are You Listening?	23
17-C Bah Hum Bug!	24
Fickle Eyes	25
Only Here	26
Gassed Up & Gassed Out	27
Piffle	28
Morse Code	30
Base Gong	31
Prozac One	32
Vicadin Bitch	33
Dr. Yunnus Laughs	34
Ticker Tape Parade	35
Dormant Skies	36
The Rainbow Is a Pig	37
Liquid Mettle	38
Show Me!	39
Mrs. Shroff	40
Ninja Gilgamesh	41
Dear Lady Good Friday "The Columbia is Lost"	42
Cope with Hope	44
At 50	45
Oughtism	46
Oh! That Arrowroot! Right Now Is All I've Got	48
Please Don't Go To Sleep	50
In the End Zone	51
4:15 p.m. CA Time	52
You Stole My Daughter's Funeral	53
Prayer From A Floating Soul	54
Unpack My Boxes	55

Barnacles of the Free Soul	56
Ctrl Alt Delete < Escape ^	57
Unlearn	59
Hung Backwards	60
So Let's Start Our Own Tradition	61
Saigon & Survival	63
The Right Price	65
Kaboom	66
So Many Laps To Go	67
Unnatural(ly) Grave(s)	68
Hanging From a Bus Strap	69
To Do To Be	71
Rules Are For the Birds	73
Our Piece of Mahabalipuram Here in San Bernardino	74
A Pinch of Land	76
Eat Drink Piss Without Your Permission	77
An Orphanage Must Be Cozier	79
Rooms of Pain	81
Cookie Crumb Clichés	83
The Stuff of Hands	84
I Am Cschacschatti Woman	86
Your Veluri Literary Common Kitchen Sense	88
Aaha! That's Filter Coffee	89
Dosa Delight	90
Spiritual Sanity	91
Little Telugu Women of the Earth	92
"Injoy"	97
Svabhimaanam	101
The Man In the Moon	102
Oh Look, Tsunami Tsunami	104
"Dilli Durbar"	105
H1 Bliss: Let it Be	107
Colonial Sell Out	110
Physician Heal Thyself	111
"Canyugis"	112
www.opportunity.ca.us	114
The Eye of the Storm	116
And so Spot Said to Fido	117
And so the Stupid Critic Said	118
Hung Out ^On a Shingle	119
Change	122
My Mumbai Oh! My Mumbai	123
About the Author	127

San Bernardino Passion

Bite into the slushy passion of the persimmon out here
and sink into the orange membranous skies of San Bernardino
its fully barbecued forest fires, its chocolaty mudslides.
When its skin is taut and ready to go

Oooooooo eeeeeeee Ooooooo eeeee –

it's persimmon passion alright,
bite into San Bernardino and it will bite back.

San Bernardino Blues

Tharan thara
Tharan thara
Thud Schtlick
Tharan thara
Thud Schtlick

Sombrero on head,
he shovels the brown desert earth
nurtured by his blood his pus
from an infected hangnail —

the piss
the shit

some more piss some more shit
of passing migrants
tilapiaed into rust bucket trucks.

In a long bloodline
his *Tonala Mehican* melodies
torn from his guts deep beneath the navel
where true music breathes
rise through the sticky
web of thick Valencia groves,
skip a spiny beat,
twist in the smog for a jiffy
pretzeling up
to slap the dirty egg yokey spidery veins
of Mojave clouds
spattered against the placenta sun
doughy and salty,
a shitty hot mess.

Vested in his sweated lime green
construction orange strapped armor
in the midst of a drubbing workday—
with a flick of his wrist
a doggy kick of his thighs
uncontained timber,
he grunts tunelessly —

Tharan thara
Tharan thara
Thud Schtlick

to a Death Valley beat.

Uvulaic Rhapsody

The Santa Ana
banshees by.
Double paned glass windows shudder
to the brink of cracking,
then stiffen up, double barred,
secured, locked down
in Barstow Norco Devore.
By dawn, by dusk, the brown-grey ash
crucibled to perfection, filters eerily
into the frills of every dainty pillow
scrunches the bubbles of semen hocked
mattresses —
For life.
The follicles are rooted by it.
Crunchies bead on the tongue.
Dust bowls pocket the back of the throat
no chilled Tecate can irrigate.

Dirt Devil all you want.
In the Cajon Pass
this giant uvulaic rhapsody goes on.

And Then the Mountain Dies

Those Caterpillars, man, they tear up
whole mountains,
whole hearts, whole lives buried
deep within the soul
of San Bernardino. They suck it out
and up where once
their humble namesakes,
the humble earthworms
and caterpillars turned the fresh soil
not yet woken from
its dewy night slumber, so the marigolds,
the wildflowers, the startled hares,
the butterflies could pop out of the earth
and wish it well.

Those Caterpillars, man, they're hungry
to flatten the mountain,
to chew up the rattlesnakes,
the mounds of dusty soil
trapped in raspy breath, only
the Cajon Pass could scare up.

Those Caterpillars, man, can watch while
the whole mountain dies under
their combined treads.
They're hungry to taste the new life beneath
their rolling teeth. Like the Burbanites
they stand to serve, they carve up the land the soil,
the heart of San Bernardino, which watches
while another mountain dies.

The Arsonist: Halloween Masquerade

He squatted at the I-18 & 173 crossroads
to ease his billion $ itch
and caught the Santa Ana *firenado*
at its balsy peak —

Whoooooooooooosh

7 miles per minute
as the dazed smoke
clenched every valley
in fits of ashy whirls,
as mothballed memories
sparked about
and the Golden State turned ashen.

I Burn You Burn We All Burn Together

My personal piece of heaven disoriented by grief
that the weight of tears does not relieve, minute to minute,
June 22, you bobcat, from your starship in memoriam,
from your Libran lair graze the Arrowhead mountain range
at last, so that I can finally feel close to you,
our wonderful memories of love laughter and light,
vibrant with verve and vigor in these hunkered down
hairy, nappy, San Bernardino mountains,
to relieve the bullet ridden firing range cardboard cutout
memories of pain of one dead, *oh,* so before her time.

Yet I cannot save my personal piece of heaven here.

A good man's evacuation, milk and honey memories
on terra cotta roofs, now ash and dust in cranial corners,
now curling with tobacco fingered asthmatic smoke to blot out
the inert sun, darkness at noon, unmasked illusions, the cat,
the dog, the photographs, the insurance papers, the ID, the cash,
your legal self, futility jammed into a box with numb fingers
that cannot pry the jamb faster than the flames lick another
mountain crown, the brain in slow motion, so slow, so heavy,
so suppressed, so suffused with smoky realities smeared against
a neighbor's windows, grappling with banal actualities of the picket
lines at Ralph's, so crucial and demanding attention yesterday —
gone in a flick today.

The gray at noon, evacuation smolders in the soul and gives
just enough slivered wiggle-room to vacate, to slither through
the French doors as a thin slice of giddy happiness makes for
a momentous getaway on a wafer.

Clarify, simplify, shed, molt and bolt today as if the billowing
embers were upon us everyday.

The lusting power of clichés and profanity makes the heat
crystal clear in the clogged afternoon.

Carry yourself on your back.
Pack your tiny pieces of heaven.

Pack clichés dreams-photos, grandma's talisman, Vioxx,
Lipitor, oxygen tanks and masks, insulin lines.

Licks of illusion caramelized to perfection peel off
in one crust — a teardrop evaporating on a slaked cheek
like drops of water on the roaring fire. Nothing focuses
the mind like an evacuation, nothing harder than the futility
of watching our carefully nursed illusions go up in smoke.

The Columbia explosion, 9/11, now this raining down, snowy,
delusional ash, the fret and the fuss—
what the heck are we to make of all of this huh?

Get a grip now, the only reality might be in snapping
Shut the lid of the box bursting with nothingness —

Driver's license, laptops, floppies, work/school stuff,
hard realities as though anything had substance anyway,
the human heart a floppy disk hard to erase, the rich, the poor
in clotted massed pain, real pain, not the staged blown up pain
of the "Aviators" set, nor the idle jokes of the "Collectinator"
in Sacramento.

In California, *who knows* —
Our lungs gone to hell in a hand basket of a man-made rage
against the innocent skies—
Big #'s, big dreams, big hopes, for life again
here, for 729,000 acres gone in a burn, 2600 homes gone in a burn,
20 dead and still counting, across San Bernardino, San Diego,
Fontana, Santa Clarita, Claremont, Simi Valley.

Where else will it go? Where else will it go to stop?
Masses still running with botched thoughts towards the blotted sun.

This is a tragedy all right, not a competition.
The careless arsonist reminds us of our identity as he robs us of it.

At last the real snow comes, birth light, welcome drizzle,
holding the line on the mountain tops of Crestline, Cedar Glen,
Twin Peaks, Arrowhead, Running Springs and Big Bear, baby—
big California Bear snuffing out the bark beetle's insatiable thirst
for our forests.

As the black settled ash, the dysmenhorric, rotted, wet, rusted ash
in our mouths, our nostrils, our lungs our pores sediments itself into
Halloween like Phoenixes nestled in San Bernardino's Norton
Air force Base hangars where every pretense of life slaps
against the port-a-potties. Be good, look good, do good —
so the gauze pulled over our hearts, and eyes,
is somehow bearable again.

CA Witches Brew

The earth shook first
then rumbled gruffly,
rollicked about,
then convulsed,
if only for a second,
on July 29th, 2008 at 11:42 a.m.

The dazed students scattered about,
slid from their chairs
onto the helpless ground,
defenselessly,
as the lavender Earthquake plan
rattled on the wall.

So much unity, trust, loyalty in the room
banded us together in that instant.
San Bernardinans deal calmly
with the earth's treachery.

*Beat her to a pulp, the earth
and she will spit on you,*
my grandma used to say,
venomously
searching in her belly
for a split second
before spewing sulphur about.

*The Kaliyug has come
she would say.*
And so it has,
and so it will.

As phone lines jammed and CNN revolved 24/7,
Judge Judy ran like a rat taking her scissor sharp tongue
with her. The Cal Tech super seismologist blathered

in variables as the Governor chaffed at the Feds
for failing infrastructure unfit for the coast.

And so we pay our taxes never holding our breath
to hear the Chief of LA's Fire Dept. finally speak the truth.
He warns that we'd be on our own when
the Great American Ding hits.

Katrina taught us that.
Katrina taught us to be pioneering cowboys
rounding up our supplies into a tight circle of sharing,
daring the authorities to trespass.

We San Bernardinans took it so calmly,
so well — eerie.

The earth settled back into a rut
stirring her witches brew
for another time.

Maria Oh Maria

What more can I say,
Maria oh Maria.
In Barstow, Norco,
Devore, Victorville,
Colton, Rialto,
Fontana, Loma Linda,
Highlands, Redlands,
Uplands, Cajonlands,
San Bernardino,
Riverside even,
your passion etches
every floor, every banister,
every toilet, every faucet,
every shower, every tub,
every carpet, every counter,
every mattress, every pillow,
every nozzle, every knob,
every grim corner,
every womb, every tomb—
spotless virginal.
Oh where
Oh where
Art Thou
Maria oh Maria?

Shower Stall Swan Song

Goddamnit, shit all over the place,
brown shit streaking
the hammered glass shower door,
the tub's white tile
residue of a careless arse.
I mean she scrubbed and scrubbed,
then scrubbed some more,
cleaned her heart out,
got down on all fours
doggie style-just the way he liked it,
on her hands and knees,
latexed-yellow, tough-as-nails, gloved hands,
and scrubbed in the tony apartment
their steadfast shower stall
under the full weight of the Rockies,
so the stench could not get out there.
The more she scrubbed
the more there was
oozing over dollar bills,
the empty Captain Morgan's
with the voices screaming
to scrub harder,
Quicker!
Tabla Rasa.
Then her spine broke free
of her back.
Strangely pain free,
euphoric,
So she said, *No shit,*
and simply left.

Aqua American

Ethiopia blackens its scoured sores, its roots,
its nascent heartbeats on the fragile feet of flies.
The Edenic banks of Mesopotamian yore blister
the Euphrates-Tigris arteries. The Gobi desert
spawns its rigid arid canopy in Indo-Chinese wrath,
where the melting icy chills of the Antarctic
can never penetrate. Deep veined thrombosis
engorges Amazonian girth. CA, a shriveled prune,
pillages the Colorado bowl to form mirrors of dust.
Our timed sprinklers dance carelessly day after day,
nuzzling our carefully sculpted, manufactured, bold
blades of grass guzzling the deepest bowels of the plains
to the very bones of creation itself.

H_2O, H_2O everywhere.
Not a drop to drink.
Aqua American.

Cabo Cabo

Where, oh where have the Tonala gone?
Never mind them.
The eager hands reach
the Americano *Touristas* at the dusty, barbecued
airport to whisk them along miles long
Pacific Coast cruise ships, already hocked
through Sheraton Hilton *paradisoes* —
resorts with bracelets of $1000, access to
across-the-border, one-and-the-same,
genuine delights.
Never mind the Tonala.
In the beer Tequila soaked spring breaks
tagged with Walmarted, Coscoed, McD's hiss.
Motorized boats extend friendship
to the mating humpbacks in nature's arched rock
doorway, clicked to digitized perfection,
emailed the same instant.
Never mind the Tonala,
who beat back the crowds in the ribbon, downtown,
alleys where the piss and shit are hidden from poking
tourista eyes amid shanty-shops, the soft, floppy, deer-skin
leather, tan, smooth, scented with the hand-crocheted,
organic vegetable-colored designs of yore.
Never mind the Tonala.
She works till midnight with her 3rd grader
on the shop floor, sprawled school books everywhere
scoffing at becoming the President someday.
Will be a doctor one day.
Never mind the Tonala.

Loins On the Line

Change schmange. One's a blustering fool. The other a blubbering
idiot. One's just old Kennedy juice in a new bottle, a twitter.com—
the other a Reaganesque-Bushist fizzled Molotov. Puny fish
in a big old pond itching to be whales, grande froth rising to the top,
just desperate men for desperate times impalin' us on their creeds.
Gravitas is for us idiots, for July 4th. Our Flag.
It's not about the elitism.
It's not about the symbolism.
It's not even about their shit-soaked platitudinisms.
July 4th. Our Flag.
Republican rabidity, Democratic
demagoguery, take your pick—the lesser of the two evils passing
for democracy. Time to throw the "change" and its chumps
down the every-vote-counts-crap-coagulated drain of 2-party
strangulation.
July 4th. Our Flag.

Ask them whose loins are on the line.
Ask them. For them it is torn flesh, desert sand in every crack
of their dreams, sentient immigrant skulls with the flag coiled,
tourniquet-tight around purple, marooned hearts.
July 4th. Our Flag.

Hey Emma, Are You Listening?

Not your stump speech, not your whistle stop, not even
your Teddy Truman crap. Some truth then, only shadings
of it now, 60 second tv spots, on Cookinglight.com,
Dr. Phil and Oprah, or blasts from hell on rave&rant.com,
negative bile on the front page, honeyed drool on the last
of even graying mouthpieces, the New York Times, CBS,
minutiae that shakes the Beltway, blurred vision shoots
right through CBS to Fox, Tivo past the headlines—
they're all the same.

Wipe the slate clean and start all over again
only to have the bile spit at you in the eye.

Every 4 years two guys stand up proud, or so it seems,
over and over, mouthing heresies, over the Machiavellian
spinmeisters. It is so because I think so.
I believe so, or is it because I am convinced it is so?
Who knows? Who cares? Should we?

So roll up your carpet of lies and please go home.
Think up more plausible lies so I can vote my considerable
conscience while all our neighbors think we've nazi'd up.
If democracy is a two-headed monster heading straight
for the good old dust heap — *the lesser of two evils?* you say.
Brother, spare me a dime.

Hey Emma, are you listening?
Hi ho, let the best spin win.

But what do I know— more recently arrived
with my vote clutched between my teeth?

17-C Bah Hum Bug!

Citigroup and At&T ganged up and sent me
a 17 cent check in the mail just in time for the holidays.
Hurrah!

You slick willies you-17 cents you took from my
4 part-time-jobs-single-parent, terminally-ill-disabled-child
supporting, mind-blowing, juggling household paycheck.
Monopolizing our entire neighborhoods, cowering before your
conglomerate stress, 17 cents that a class action suit against
your sorry arses forced you to cough up like the fur ball bills
you've been cramming down our throats all this time.

We knew you'd each get back next to nothing,
your irreverent letter with the 17c check said, *But nooo
we've been ordered to pay up for swindling, if you don't cash
it by xx/xx/xx, we'll just donate it to charity.*

You slick willies you, I shall frame your 17 cents for posterity
and laugh all the way to the bank with you,
so one hungry mouth may eat and weep.

Fickle Eyes

When Eliot celebrates *Dharma*, the West cheers.
When Hitler the *swasthika* distorts
the West ignorant indifference courts.
People everywhere on purposeful parole
from the eyes of the soul.

Therein lie the irreparable seeds of conflict
in the Middle East, the Wars, even the cruel 9/11
cut and now the Mumbai Massacre.
One eye open, one eye shut.

Only Here

Only here can you be both legal and illegal.
Only here can you be drizzled with ad-frenzied choices
of a new-and-improved Dawn (Heaven is it in that Dawn
to be alive) that will not strip your subcutaneous cells,
lulled by the first woman, the first black man, the first old man
running for president while she is relentlessly pushed off center.

Only here can you be Earth Day-mad for a moment
and hummer-whip her the next. Only here can the comma
lose currency to
LOL POS GTGO BTB BFF,
to "Don't taser me bro,"
while we proudly bravely throw
We're # 1, We ARE to the throngs.

Only here can you be silent while the advancing armies
employ the people's car, the Nano, slippers and lead laden toys,
only here can you wag your thick blunt finger at naughty China,
naughty India, only here can you condemn, uplift, roar in laughter
at your backyard beef barbecue, only here can you mess up,
dress up the truth, 'fess up, press up against the dank, dinghy
synapses of your skull your soul, only here can you lean against
the world, brave and free, only here can you wave the 50 stars
and thirteen stripes while your tooth brush loses
hair every day.
Only here.

Gassed Up & Gassed Out

    NIMBY bro

Nimby.

Let's ship 'em all back to wherever they crawled out from —
Chiquita Republics, Madarasas, Gulags, Gas Ovens,
(Can I even say that can I even think that?)
Veldts, or even jungles.

Heck, I'm American.
I can slide into my Hummer anytime, in fact. I can slide
into my Sequoia, Yukon, Tahoe, Tundra, F 250, Vera Cruz.

Hey bro,
I'm the Pathfinder, I'm the Explorer, I'm the frigging Navigator
Escalading through the border to get my gas for $ 2.85 —
while all across *Mehico* there is a drought of stunted, dried up
gas stations hobbled by American pride.

And the Chicanos wave, *Go Home Yanqui* signs
in my backyard in a fit of reverse discrimination.
We're sure as hell gassed up & gassed out.

Piffle

Hi ho hi ho,
we're rotten to the core — silent strained Rockies against
the cowboy sky, Phat Daddy sexambulating his hips
to a croon, the Highlanders perambulating around the pool,
veneers of diversity, well done on the skin, dripping with chocolate
brown A1 sauce, bleeding pink tender raw at the bone, striated
cellulose moving butt on the floor, as the wheelchair-liberated
gyrate near the accessible door, averted eyes, sidling steps
towards sunshine gleaming Beamers, Rams, ML 320's,
Mustangs, the secluded
western pioneering beat, moaning,
Shiva Shiva Shiva Shiva
Rama Rama Rama Rama
Hi ho hi ho,
we're rotten to the core.

White fish pale fat oozing out of swimsuits, stretch marks
across brown virgin breasts swarming out of straight jackets,
bikini thongs, prematurely scratched against softly heaving bellies,
grazing the salads the sodas. You give up what for what.

Phat Daddy — now crooning on the floor, pelvyrating
along with slathered ice cream cones, frothing
with pent up ecstasy, as always, the Rockies scrunched
screaming semen soaked sheets with Boulder's *Sherpas*
flattening their noses against the blunt sky—
come plant our summer flowers, heave transplanted
torn evergreens to go home to the foothills nudging
those hulking mountains, and smoke dope
with your brothers while cockroaches ransack
the kids' dreams with Payday loans, Pawn sharks,
the Liquor Marts who piss *Tecate*, Tequiza, then Patron
on their neighbors' front doors in rainbow colors,
and come hither to the Ranch through the gate
to do your solemn landscaping, duty swaddled

in red blue and white
no place here at this pool party. But we do want your hands,
fingers raw to the pinkish joints, choking on fumes
and chemicals, scrunched Rockies semen
screaming,
Hi hi hi ho,
we're rotten to the core.

The silent Rockies salute the sky, celebrate the sky
spiritualize the sky, sentinels to straying spirits
all about the land, surface happy,
Hi ho hi ho,
we're rotten to the core.

Go on and on
The mountains don't care. The pork bellied golfers
hiding their red necks that peep through Lacostes,
steeples jostling minarets, temples keeping the soul tightly
sealed in,
Allah Ho Akbar Allah
Praise the Lord
Shiva Shiva Rama Rama
the Rockies don't care,
Hi hi hi ho
we're rotten to the core.

Morse Code

Inside
Black and blonde,
Southern Baptist
Hindu, Shaiviite,
Northern, Southern, Unitarian,
gathered to bless this union.

Two narrow sides of the two aisles ablaze with rigid color –
here murky blue, royal navy blue, marigold, burnt orange,
Malabar, Romani, mangoed, hollowed-out gold, mighty garnet
reds, hibiscus-honeyed swirls of threads, *Gul mohr*-splayed
hues – royal green, purple, maize, peacock brown, jaundiced yellow,
silent, heavy *Kanchi* silks, screaming blind dots liberally sprinkled
on attendant foreheads here—spewing rock hard vows. There-
punishing pastels, petulant pouting petunia, primrose-jaded greens,
ground-down glorious peach, creamy, split gauzy egg-white timorous
taffeta, the coupling of Southern American organza and Southern
Indian silk at the altar, struggling, bargaining, seeking, up in the dome
of rafters, the choking fumes of *gheed* incense, pigeon-holed balance
of champagne chilled, silver, golden fishbowl expectations spill out,
chill out, calm out, shroud out, demeaning, disgusting, encrusting,
ennobling stiff joints of entropy *till death do us* cast.

Outside –the lone squirrel holds erect amidst compost of thistle
thorn and thrush, tapping out the mating-Morse Code,
pockmarked with corrosive condoms, cellulose diapers, gelatinous
catheterized noses of domestic hush
unto eternity, drizzled, drenched, composted love.

60-40
20-80
10-90
decode, uncode
click click click click
scramble, unscramble.

Base Gong

Feel sick in your skin constipated to the gills with guilt,
burdened with conditional love, with no free flow,
blood clotted joy, dammed up, all that *karma* crap,
schizophrenic caterwauling, a clinical crescendo,
the base gong
that bolts the nuts of pain down,
screwed so tight
the deathbed pops with platitudes,
deathbed joke of forgiveness
a shameless bid for heaven.

New vocabulary
GIA: Go It Alone
MYMB: My Arse My Business
GIG: Guilt in Gaiety
IKB: I Know Best
GEG: Get a Grip
Base gong.

It's not in the pots of gold.
It's not in the goose pimply scarce rainbows.
Right here right now, with guilt scarring and sticking
out the spine, mothering is in tying the shoelaces.

Prozac One

I used to be giddy for life
now I'm just dizzy and dopey
thanks to Pfizer and my doctor (Pfoctor!).
My strangled sense of self
boiled away to the bone,
I gave my life to work
and work took *my* life
dicing *my* core
into open folders
the marrow of sacrifice
stashed in MY Briefcase
in MY Documents
in Penn Station.
So I jog into the sunset sometimes.
The world needs me.

Vicadin Bitch

Surgeon dearest
could you please
shave and scoop this god awful
pain out
so I can stop
being so loose as a goose
on Vicadin
so I can look up
look down
again
hold my regal carriage
again
sniff just the skies
the grass
again
mitochondrial recovery
rich-bitch, witch.

Dr. Yunnus Laughs

Poof goes the balloon taking IndyMac with it, 95 poofs and counting all over my 'hood alone, uncut lawns sprouting wilted weeds of dreams —
Bank Owned.

Gramm chastises — *A nation of whiners.*
Michelle Obama intones — *Stimulus package for a pair of earrings.*

Upside down mortgages, inside out smiles, charred over speculative shoulders, shrugging off sub prime landscapes.

Fannie Mae, Freddie Mac, poof!
Bear & Stearns, Lehman Brothers, AIG poof!
Government compatriots, so just like Chrysler,
oooh not so long ago, bail outs reserved for its lackeys,
while modest lawns get browned, more burned.

Call it what you will, Darwinian soothsayer, naked greed does us all in on those brown burnt lawns in those reed-choked swimming pools.

Trust, loyalty.
Microcredit anyone?
Dr. Yunnus Laughs
All the way to and from the bank.

Ticker Tape Parade

Wink & blink,
the ticker tape blinks
-273.72.
The ticker tape winks
+ 82.23.
Day in and day out
stagflation chokes
the abandoned bank owned lawns.

Thoughts swirl out of pure chaos
forming, shaping,
mud wrestling unformed words
as they jump, leap,
writhe, with a flick of serrated tails,
into pure poetry.

The one overvalued,
the other undervalued,
while our small lives
whirl in an eddy of oil and food,
usurped,
devalued.

Dormant Skies

American Air inched grudgingly forward
on runway LC 69
with its flock of
secured, screened, debuttoned, deshoed, debriefed,
descissored, declawed, defanged, delotioned,
debauched on freedom, security, and peace—
cargo—
safe in their sealed seats,
elated at saber rattling pilots,
with magnums aloft,
cockpit doors Fort Knoxxed,
beards, turbans, singing shoes
of all colors and sizes
remanded.
Heathrow, a hotbed of honeyed horrors
throbbed again.

Debugged   Detoxed   Denumbed
Defrocked   Desiliconed   Decorked
Dedrugged   Debotoxed   Dedumbed
Debased—
Out of the cockpit,
nude.

The Rainbow Is a Pig

The rainbow is a pig.
It tantalizes
without any pot of gold
at the beginning, middle, or end.
Yet I crave its
verdigris deceit.
Does that tell you
more about me,
the artful rainbow
or our corrugated dreams?
Pots of gold
ground
in our hearts and heads.

Liquid Mettle

The rat said to the mouse,
"Believe."
The mouse said to the rat,
"YOU Believe!"
The certainty of science
collided
with the certainty of faith.
The common ground shifted
spinning into liquid mettle.
Atrophy.
Entropy.

Show Me!

God gazes over the addled crowd
rich with champagne and chocolate
'till the fizzy bubbles pop
in the back of their throats
tingling the fine thready nostril hairs,
firing up an orgasmic attunement
that courses through the dull veins,
the morose nipples in the house,
where the old men hit on the fillies.

God gazes over this effetedom,
jumping up 'n down,
yelling.
"Show me, show me, show me."

Raise your glasses Wonder Women all,
raise them high
and show me,
in a conspiracy of tolerance,
that I am more than just the bombs
converting people to hate to faith
asking meekness—

That I am more
much more than all this
in this House.
Wonder Women of the world
raise your glasses
at this hour
to a conspiracy of tolerance
and show me.

Mrs. Shroff

Punctual	Shepherdess
Courteous	Abiding
Indefatigable	Inculcating
Dedicated	Humane
Committed	Passionate
Scholarly	Convincing
Grammatical	Believing
Epigrammatic	Respectful
Succinct	Absorbing
Topical	Influential
Meticulous	Rigorous
Righteous	Universal

        Indefatigable

Fifth grade vocabulary
tossed like a salad for success,
today ratemyprofessor.com
would deem "brutal and brilliant".

Mrs. Shroff —
kindling and rekindling souls
then and forever
so we could go out to kindle too.

Ninja Gilgamesh

Then the glorious Gilgamesh asked
the gasping *Enkidu*,
"If 99% is just stuff 1% the real deal,
why try and try if I'm gonna die,
for real."

...Oh
Try and try coz I'm gonna die?
Didn't get that
in the nick of time
Kurt Cobain
whatever
nor you Heath Ledger
seriously.
Joker.

Dear Lady Good Friday "The Columbia is Lost"

(Tribute In Memoriam to Mrs. Linda Grace Hoyer Updike)

"The Columbia is Lost," gone in a Haley's pop,
shshshshshshshshshsh, scalding the debrised souls of nations
over CA, AZ, TX, searing cockles of the pod cocoon of seven
searching, zig-zaggy stars— floating, mindful, reasoned, cohesion,
sterile, subdued, sane, sealed, multi-foliate rose, unglued, stewed,
heated tossed offhand, shafting, splintering smithereens,
flaming, bleeding, brittle pigeon feathers,
charismatic, Catholic, Baptist, Christians, Hindu, Jew—
shshshshshshshshshshshshshshshshshshshshsh
"The Columbia is Lost" intones the voice
as the chaplain of the benediction also intones —
"Those who have accepted Christ as savior will go to heaven."

How did it come to be so? Tis in Heaven
as it is on earth Dear Lady Good Friday?

I turned off that "pink" dirt-road turnpike
95 times in my head, in quilted Reading, PA,
golden dust gathering in the corners of my cranium,
so many moons ago, where your homestead,
your farm, your dogwood tree, are still there
resting in oblivion.

You filled the door frame with your genial humor,
(George tethered in the backyard) amiably inviting me in to tea,
welcoming my brown heathen, wheat-complexioned countenance,
colonial, my encounter, nativistic challenger of maximum thrust,
"we are go at throttle up!" all in reverse to embrace my new land,
cross the new frontier, endeavor, pioneer. Through your generosity,
your hospitality, your democracy, your "benighted" not besotted,
your survival of your depression, your world wars, your ivy leagues,
your marriage, your birth, a whole new deal, your suffering suffragist
swath,

your books, published & unpublished, your tolerance,
your farm, your Buick Skylark, regal, real, your dentist,
your stable, your lawn, tended, real, your precious son,
gone just now in January 09, your wit, your grace homespun,
your politics, your peace, ahoyer, your human flesh & bone,
your laughter, your ceaseless friendship in lovely Dutch letters,
seeded single, on Good Friday, and every one thereafter,
your phone calls, only before/after "Guiding Light",
your pneumonia, your hospital, your letterquette, real,
still very much there, your scope, your depth, your brea(d)th,
Centaurish, your compassion unfailing, abiding, flexing,
inviting year after year, your etched, dried signature
on my bones, still beaconing me past the floundering
timorous stabs at the mundane, your presence,
your (g)race, your smooth velvety gaze, moored,
are still there with me, golden dust,
in the corners of my cranium.

Dear Lady Good Friday
Today
Now.

So what happened to all of that, Dear Lady?
So how has it come to be so, Dear, Dear Lady Good Friday
that The Columbia Is Lost?

Cope with Hope

Dedicated to TRISHA MEILI, Central Park Jogger. Presented to her at the CA Governor's National Conference for Women on 22nd October, 2003 at the Long Beach Convention Center).

Inspired by Trisha Meili, ancient East Indian texts and poems, and John Donne's "Batter My Heart.

Batter and bruise my body
batter and bruise my heart
batter and bruise my body
batter and bruise my heart
all night long
here, there, everywhere
in the entrails of the park
till the kernel of my soul
coiled tightly in the dark
springs back
yet another life to start.

Shantih, Shantih, Shantih.

At 50

At 50
my tits are tilted heavenwards
proudly,
so quit talking to them.
Duty is in the details
and they're done with those —
getting the baby,
feeding the baby,
into joyful survival.
That's *all*.
now I wish for them to be still,
to go away,
at each mammogram
simply test negative,
that's ALL.

Oughtism

Pirouette,
joy birds flapping wings —
happy, happy bird day
yappy, yappy,
throw,
flap,
twirl,
lick lick lick lick lick lick lick lick lick lick,
rubber plastic metal,
mommy's face, *yum yum, yummy,*
mommy's major, major *no no*—
The bear went over the mountain,
round and round the mulberry bush,
the prickly pear, the prickly pear,
yeh, baby, yeh
clap, clap, clap—
If you're happy and you know it,
down the slide,
go, go, go.
Wisdom in the pirouette
in the circle—
ecstasy.

Then there's the mommy fluff.
making it real.
making it last.
simplicity. clarity.
Long, long days
silent night.
99% stuff, 1% the real deal.
Labors of love,
studded in nails,
in coffins,
hold, hold, hold,
onto the slivers of truth, of light.

When you wish upon a star
it falls to earth.

Can I
Can I
Oughtism.

Oh! That Arrowroot! Right Now Is All I've Got

Falling apart at the seams, shattered to the bone,
clenching onto a wisp of will for that big thing upstairs
in the baby's room, drifting away with atrophying,
botoxed muscular tendons, taut with sinotic emblems
of measured time. I'm panicking, her mama—

*"Oh Susie, come quick, I need salt and oil,
vegetable oil, to fix my favorite foods,
and I've run out, 'coz I'm marooned here
in sharp breathing, quick Susie,
I have to fix my favorite foods
the way grandmamma used to
or I can't manage, I can't cope."*

Have to fix that arrowroot, that *arabi that chamadumpa
right now*, as the baby would say, the way mamma used to fix it,
growing up all those years before she went crying out for me
in her waning thrombotic moments, must fix them just the way
she did, the arrowroot *arabi chamadumpa*, pressure cooked
to magnificent tenderness before I shuck their loose sage, brown,
bearded, goat-like splotched faces to reveal their soft yet firm
whites slipping around in their slimy juices of life, ah,
the aroma of heaven itself descends and grabs me by the throat,
Mamma's brass family *kadai*, sizzling, ready with oil
hungry for the half moons to be thrown in and tossed till
golden brown crisp jackets envelope soft tender inner hearts
just a hint of fresh ground *dhaniyam jeera and asofoetida*
carelessly drizzled over the bubbling golden orbs, out
they come over fresh cooked, sticky rice, glazed with *ghee*,
oh Mamma, they reach across the ancestral gap with spicy
richness, Grandma's kitchen wisdom, that even a bull can
fix fried food, but not this kind of heaven, consoling even
in this spasm of pain, wafting upstairs as she prepares to depart

and join the rest, as I devour my concoction that reaches
over this ancestral gap, hungrily with hot soft oozing, bright
yellow turmeric *daal,* scalding my fingers, my tongue, my taste buds ,
just the way good food should be eaten, you'd say. Eat up and go up
to lose my one and only baby.
Right now is all I've got.

Please Don't Go To Sleep

Hush 'lil baby
don't go to sleep
Mama has to hear
your heartbeat
above the beep

Keep a wretch like me
safe and warm
my 'lil angel
from the storm

I know it's supposed to be
the other way around
my dying daughter
I too am barely above the ground

My 'lil petunia
now up above
so tiny so shiny
so bright with love.

Shantih, Shantih, Shantih.

In the End Zone

Wailing from deep within my womb
in fits and starts
you tear through your placental memory
into your new reality
in your end zone.

Rasping breath from deep within your faltering lungs,
in fits and starts,
you clutch onto your cranial memory
with blue extremities
in the end zone.

All of this, caught on tape,
book-ending your brief life
for this maternal, wallet-memory
which, for five years after you flickered out,
livens each minute, each day, each year,
into my end zone.

4:15 p.m. CA Time

I took my daughter's death standing up,
my head held high,
my shoulders squared,
knuckles grief-gripping the chair,
with sob-clogged pores,
though the voice at the end of the line
bullied me into sitting down.
4:15 p.m. CA time,
the day was long,
the hands on the clock short,
my heart heavy with love,
pressure crawling up
my coiled spine,
as she and I had grabbed onto those
hands—
in breath, in death.
I STILL AM.

You Stole My Daughter's Funeral

You stole my daughter's funeral,
her cremation,
her last rites.
What's the matter with you?
Silently she went in the end,
all purple and blue.

By your absence, your presence,
you stole my daughter's funeral,
her cremation,
her last rites.
What's the matter with you?

Pick your nose out of your navel
and look all around you,
see me, her mother, cry.
Look up and see the blue sky
to respect the ones that truly die.

Prayer From A Floating Soul

Dear Lord God, please have mercy,
and descend from on high,
to meet me where I am, right now
caught midstream like a floating soul,
from your mountain dwelling on high
Dear Lord God,
please descend and meet me where I am.

Dearly beloved Mother of us all,
                                    Ain't no mountain high enough,
Dear Mother Goddess, (Alimelu Manga),
                                    Ain't no valley low enough.
I just cannot even see
your Lord God's bright feet right now,
Mother of us all (Amma),
Mother of us all (Amma),
please whisper my heartfelt plea in our Lord God's ear,
for where I am right now,
                             RESPECT.
I cannot make the arduous ascent up the seven difficult mountains,
to envision his Lord God's (Venkateswara's) splendiferous Holiness.

Dear Lord God, please have mercy on me,
                              Silent night, holy night,
and descend from on high
                              All is calm, all is bright
to meet me where I am right now
                              Round yon virgin mother & child,
caught midstream like a floating soul,
                              Sleep in Heavenly peace,
a floating soul, a floating soul, a floating soul.
                              Sleep, sleep, sleep.

Unpack My Boxes

I have tried, diligently, conscientiously
for a memorably long time to unpack my boxes piled high
in the tall, tall mirrored closet, brown taped, square, small,
big, squat boxes, that compact even breathing, that rustled
first, then rasped and rattled to a morphined close
under sunny skies of a vale with not a spot of cloud
speckling the June 22 blue that absorbed me into its seething
belly, where nothing prepared me
for my child going into the ground before me.

So here I sit now—
helpless, slack jawed, the big, small tears
drizzling, drenching me, inside, outside, intensely,
those brown boxes of blood, not bony breaths taken,
with a whiff of vanilla, those Pediasure lines hanging
from the metal tripod, electronic witness to machined,
slivered-timed, g-tubed feedings, with botoxed, inflexible
tendons released into stiff socks, with a whiff of nocturnal
Nivea, a blue-black-toed sinotic finish,
for a life so preciously young.
Immortal imprints in oblivion.
Baby breath forever trapped in these tears that trickle
down my scared, scuffed, heart.

The flawless certainty of pain, learning to not come
unglued every time I lose the precious, over and over again,
'till the spine sticks out my back, with C1-8 vertebral
lasting, herniated, bulging hurt, and strength
becoming the bone that hasn't broken yet, so I come undone
and I don't unpack my dead baby's boxes.

Barnacles of the Free Soul

Unblinkered, unmuzzled, free spirited, untarred
dreams of an unchained soul, initiated at 3 by a visionary proudly
independent Dad (so his mom and my mom said "just like him"
she crowed, she fretted).

I went on to be wildly happy, soaring above the tiny irrelevancies
of life, the socially sanctioned narcissism of marriage that blinkers
the eyes to the navel, to look into the eyes of my dying child,
who seized the "right now" of life, the always "light on" joy,
to squeeze its every last dregs of hilarious absurd, giddy "yappiness,"
conjoined parent-both mother father all the time —
notgoodenough —
for anyone, anytime— each day, each minute, each second
amidst the trauma the tragedy I've lost, in a second, that proud Dad.

I've lost over a slow burn of time my beautiful special girl.
They both suck.
Now free to roam above it all above
the barnacles of my soul,
my heart, my lips,
I AM FREE.

Ctrl Alt Delete < Escape ^

Can't be anyone's rock anymore
too busy making my own rocks pebbles stones
without the acid reflux the agitation,
the shenanigans of sight and sound,
photographic memories of debris, of building the temp file
>*The folder* <*My Documents* >*My Portfolio*,
carpal tunnel vision,
with that one key in that one *Up*^ Down,
that one gasp that one lock,
saving every 5 minutes every 2 every 1,
life brushing me by,
the marrow in the elbows of my soul,
inoculated indoctrinated,
Ctrl Alt Delete,
you will lose all unused information
every 5 minutes every 2 every 1.

Are you saved?
Ctrl Alt Delete
Escape unclog soundless
the uncongealed marrow of those bones
warmly sucked and dragged,
hitting the back of my throat,
surprised amazed,
at the bloody, orangey thick, spicy plasmic sinews of each dawn
each dusk, cartilage crimson, criss-crossed, cross wired,
dyes of gelatinous skies, pink platelets, maybe splotched,
underdone, raw, ready to be sucked and dragged,
deep vein thrombosis of those drainpipes in the brain,
my state of mind my state of being my state.

Escape <
Netzero
Om
inhale exhale,

suck and drag,
and that's all there is to it,
can't be anyone's rock anymore,
too happy making my own rocks, pebbles, stones.
Now run off and make your own.

Unlearn

Unlearn
unpack
un deterred
relearn
repack
deterred
mostly deterred
a voice limns the spine
clear as a bell
very slowly
very very slowly
irrelevant first
irreverent
flawed
clear as a bell
shooting straight up the spine
the voice
eventually
ultimately
you.

Hung Backwards

Cogitate
cogitate
meditate
elevate
$c^2m=e$.

So Let's Start Our Own Tradition

And so it went, day by day, age by age, the braiding ceremony
of modesty, of grace, in center court in full view of the adoring sky,
the sticky thick perfume of coconut oil on ladylike scalps
that mummy massaged before school each morning caressing
the lustrous fronds into tapestried plaits, lock step, lock step,
'till they hung on each side of my head,
with the weight of generations.

Photographs attest to their luscious plumpness,
black as the raven's butt,
but Mummy could not control my shrieks,
as the unkind comb ripped through my matted horns,
and my veins popped in my forehead
from the grip of custom.

So Mummy muttered, helpless: "Born mouth first,
vonti pilli raakaasi, pottla chettu — she-devil, dances
to her own beat, always".

So Daddy said, "Don't ever deny, trivialize, belittle, curtail,
then dismiss her pleas."

"So let's start our own tradition," he said.

The next day she took up the grave tradition by habit, admiring
her handiwork in my oily slicked shanks, and went to stir the pot
when Daddy stepped swiftly to my side. The glint of heavy scissors
breathing down my neck—

khrr khrr

It sounded like a throat clearing phlegm as my right braid twisted,
resisted, jumped in its blade, then fell as a mass to the floor,
writhing in a whirl.

Mummy spent the whole morning then balancing the old
with the new as the new was too uneven to process.

And so our new tradition took flight.

snippety snip, khrr khrr

in the blink of a scissor cut, well ahead of its time, for all little girls
and women everywhere —a bob cut I wore
from then on,

I still do.

Saigon & Survival

So Daddy said
the wooden crate
is ready
to be shipped
to Timbuctoo
with you in it,
all of 4 stubborn years old.

So Daddy said
the darting snake,
valiantly scared,
is ready
to be fried
and spiced
in Saigon
when still Indochine
before the Americine
valiantly scared
went in
and Ho Chi Minh
ever came out.

So Daddy said
a blade of grass,
tough and eastern,
is ready
to be fried
and spiced,
splotched
with all that
spilled young blood.

So Daddy said,

continued...

"Eat up.
The plate of *dal* and rice
is ready
and eat it you will
all of 5 stubborn years,
eat it you will
without dumping it
in the neighbor's yard
before the sly cat wakes you
licking your hardened fingers
frozen shut in it."

So Daddy said,
"I went a boy, came back a man."
They are ready
to take you on,
so take them on
or they will peel you
like a banana
to stick your sinewy guts
on an over ripe
flagpole,
and stop just short
of violence dear girl,
so your rubber band,
spiral spine
is ready
to shift and flex,
without sticking
pieces of flesh and bone
over an unsuspecting
folding chair.

The Right Price

Go in
buy it,
go in,
buy it.
It's all one price anyway,
the Right Price.

All under $ 9.99–
cheaper than the Walmarted bargain
only so gorgeous
on the outside,
all the time
it shields
the frothing pain inside.

Clothes do make the face,
all of the time,
and make
suffering look so easy,
all of the time,
so Mummy said,
all of the time.
Why tell them,
if they don't know
where you got it,
how much you didn't pay for it
so long as it is smooth as silk?

Kaboom

Drink & drive,
you knock the nuts off someone
sure as hell.
The last I remember,
the army truck hurried towards us.
My Daddy belted out
"Mujhe kehte hein kallu ka val kallu ka val,"
roughly translated from the Hindi,
"You may say I am a fool, an idiot even,
but you and I will have
everlasting love,"
before he gasped his last
through a scrunched windshield,
my ragdoll Mummy at his side,
spending the past seared 44 years,
finding a way to say,
 "I love you" again.
He went in a flash,
his watch survived *forever*.
Ten years later,
no court martial in hell
fixes that.
As sure as hell
the sky went opaque on us.
Drink and drive,
you knock the nuts off someone.
There is NO responsible drinking BUD.

So Many Laps To Go

You went, clutching your bleeding heart
before I remember laying my head in your lap,
on the grassy knoll, after the drunk ngo rammed
our spanking new car at the crossroads —
still dangerous after 44 years
Daddy, you died after trying to save Saigon
from itself.

You went after I remember laying my heart in your lap,
crying out for me in the night, long after I had left
for the States, lying thrombosed in your bed of death,
at home, lying thrombosed in my bed of death,
after miscarrying in a hospital here
I heard you in my veins,
Mamma.
Daddy's mom,
you died trying to call me to your side.

How can I try now, with so much regret,
with so much pain, so many lost laps, so many tangled
veins that bind us in brave blood lines, clot lines,
so each day the mind body soul hurt somewhere,
sometime all the time.

So off to the mountains I go each dawn, to lay my head
in your lap, a soft cloud soaked lap with the light of life
filtering through into my heart, to reclaim a little piece of heaven
so I may hurt a little less each dawn, each dusk,
be happy for a spell,
so many laps to go,
so many, many more laps to go.

Unnatural(ly) Grave(s)

Trauma & drama all mushed up in your belly
and spit out in easy intervals, decade upon decade
unnatural(ly) grave(s), all of 4, and already tired
of being told they wanted a son, not you, another
girl, all of 8 years watching Daddy tourniqueted
on a grassy knoll, dead upon impact from a
soon-to-be-court-martialed, thoughtless, drunk,
his last singing, tone deaf tunes, now his morgue-tagged
toe, mom plastered into a long coma, and rehab, for
a get-your-life-together drill, skull redone with plates,
nails and flesh from everywhere, so there will be no
orphans milling around, siblings raked over for life,
preying "uncles" of all stripes, feigning father figure-hood,
"relatives" all, one initiating the others into
furtive malevolence, hounded for the nightly ritual bed
pissing of the buried shame and pain, uncontrollably,
unconsciously, 60 year old skeletal remains,
crushed into your 32 year frame, watching, waiting
to prevail over spousal carnage in scarring bipolar mundanities,
the second one full of ADHD furtive realities, scouring you
out, every way they can, well intentioned, misguided Mom
on her strong knees, beseeching them to stay, even after
the cops have come and held their sway, even though
he's hell bent on taking your name away, 40ish and your
10½ year old baby gal in her unnatural grave already,
so little life etched, so much life etched into your bones,
incisive images forged by lasting pain.

It all comes around but once.
Suddenly snatches Daddy, slowly snatches baby,
suddenly sucks, slowly stinks, not many options
on the brink. You're making a go of it,
laughing into the wind, laughing into the wind,
so you're brave — unnatural(ly) grave(s).

Hanging From a Bus Strap

Oh where, oh where have my dear lungs gone
as I search maraud for breath in this lonely serrated
cubicle, Super Mom before my time—

hanging at home by a thread of continuity
conjoined parent-both mother and father all the time
notgoodenough for anyone anytime,
hanging from the sweat stained leather strap
of the big red and yellow bus that dozes me out
to miss my stop—
again
½ hour late, again, at the darkened hour—

Hanging between the grocery load weighing down
my damaged left arm, and my stuffed work bag
suspended on my one and only working right arm,
no balance here.
This, not this, for my, kids-my daughters, and son,
not this—
Home now, stuffy and still only to repeat myself again,
4:30 a.m. — 11:30 p.m. the next day—

Hanging at work because I'm reminded
in an over-and-over-again drone —
"you're displacing a worthy man"
though my 4 hungry mouths (including mine) at home
scratch a very different story—

Hanging at work on blackened teeth, reddened eyes
soggy hopes, wispy actions between billowy swirls
of the boss' butts, through ferocious lips, imported high
tar original Marlboros, had he tipped a cowboy hat
with his steel tipped boots while leaning back
on his winged chair, I'd have pushed him all the way
so I could breathe without break for just a day —

Hanging onto my $ 80/- a month, swallowing his smoke
of full-of-myself-ness, 'till my eager-eyed, helpless
only son brandishes his thoughts like a shield
to strangle him —

Goddamn the sixties, goddamn the seventies
where my worth hangs in the balance
between smoke and mirrors, between breath-sized
bites of have-'to's, and 'to-do's,
while the leather strap on the bus gets
wetter and smellier the next day.

To Do To Be

Beautiful monotony —
make the bed, tuck the corners into even neat triangles
where nobody can even see, fold the towels into downward,
pointy triangles, scrub the hardened grout griming the tub
and pot, spray the shower curtain, now, then, so the limey spots
are camouflaged, shaded into the ground glass of routine,
pick up the shards of bread crumbs from a forgotten toaster
blackening in a drizzle the shiny porcelain veneer, dust
above, below, every which way, the fridge so corner cobwebs
get blown away, put off the garage and garden till tomorrow,
or the day after even, the laundry too.

The school bus isn't due for another hour, while the fuzz
from pets billows about.

Scrape the *to do* list clean, so you can just *be*,
in a suspended moment,
clamber upstairs, clatter down, collect your thoughts,
and keep stirring the pot.

So too marriage with its beautiful monotony.

Rules Are For the Birds

Rules are for the birds
that flock together in straight lines, in square formations,
in round inklings. I was never meant to be.
Mom 'n Dad wished for a boy, desperately aborting hope —
simply not an option then, I guess. They already had a jewel
of a first girl, who still is, and much later a perfect little boy.

Mom knocked back a *coupla* brandies for me in the womb
to still the freezing temperatures outside
so I came out hot, smooth, smacking my lips, ready
to take them on, and, boy did I ever.

From watching Dad go off to Saigon for 2 silent years
to craving his texture, his touch every day,
watching his army wife wrestle our whooping cough, measles
and mumps herself—

From being the only 8 year old witness to his gasping
last moments on that fateful grassy knoll
victim to the drunk army trucker, hoisted on his own,
court-martialed petard ten years later, when my Dad's mom
and mine lost their minds
and bodies—

From sneaking peeks at Mom, lonesome, in her 6-month-cold-coma,
to her wheelchair vigil, near the window OT PT, then PT OT again
to her 2-year-tears, as round as the unforgiving moon,
sneezing, coughing, hiccupping, sputtering, with no hope
left in her legs, or steel wheels salted
with rusty tears, her mellifluous *Carnatic* tongue congealed
in her soul, dim and distant all laughter, with no place to go
but down—

From trusting "uncles", everyone an "uncle", rub me the wrong way,
over and over again, the way a small child should never
be rubbed, because they could, because they thought no-one
was watching as I did—

To 44 seared years before Mom could even begin to say
"I love you" to that horrid, black, Friday in April '93,
my precious girl's pediatric neurologist intoning
  "I give her 2 to 20" to live to die,
  and I said "gee thanks, that helps right about now." —

To holding her pinky through the hiccups, the coughs,
the colds, to her frail frame, her sinotic toes thinning away
in puny, hushed silences, her wasting breath, even now rattling
over the numbed, tape recorded madness—

This, after 2 sick partners, one, her father, bipolar to the skull,
the other, years later, ADHD to the marrow,
the one mesmerized by his highs his lows
the other hypnotized by hard core porn, the one barely able
get it up and keep it up, the other unable to ever keep it down,
both transfixed by thoughts in their heads, altered states,
both un-medicated 'coz I needed the lobotomy, they said—

Of course. Lives in a nutshell, tossed with providential abandon
each and every breathing, kicking minute crushing the bones,
pulverizing each step, as words and deeds stuck to my spine,
spiraling out the back, raw, ugly, spent—

To the bright star in the sky, crucible for my girl's joy above,
to knowing there is no even trajectory, from hole to hole, just
weathering, withering, with no lines, no loops, for me,
the soaring above the round pegs of sky, the square realities
of cloud, meaning free, zigzag happiness, colossal —

Rules are for the birds.

Our Piece of *Mahabalipuram* Here in San Bernardino

Oh! Daddy
come back for just a day 'coz I wonder if you remember
that last piece of *Mahabalipuram* you savored on our last
family picnic with laughing gala relatives, family, and friends,
wife 27 and three kids 10, 6, and 4, the tall sentinel pines
poking their cone laden spurs against the burning Indian sky,
patchless blue, against the hot, dry, white, oh so white, sands
licked by roaring waves, that treasure the half sunken temple
the world's best hidden Ninth Wonder,
intricately carved to *Chola* perfection.

Our piece of *Mahabalipuram* now comes across the centuries,
the decades, here, now, even in San Bernardino, before
you were frozen into the Cherian Brothers family photo frame
so handsome and debonair in your grey English suit, all propa'
with chunky black frames against your pale skin, your classic nose,
before you were frozen for all time for us, and shipped off
to Saigon in 1960, all of 31 years old, where you proudly
mediced in the trenches, patching up as much blood
as you could, staunchly to preserve your fellow men in arms,
tourniquet, amputate, drill without anesthesia,
on a steady diet of fried grass, snake and eels
'till the diarrhea excavated another hole in your behind,
and burned off what little skin was left around it,
signs of life, still there in the shrieks, when water
touched the pinkish redness.

One day when you got back, all of 35, dying, tourniqueted, yourself,
on a grassy knoll, on Pune's Prince of Wales Road,
ready for the morgue, with your now 8 year old kneeling
over you, the only family witness, to your going, not knowing
the rottenness of reality.

Your absence makes me stronger, more than the sudden, quick,
meaningless motions of those present, yammering
all the while, well meaning, unintentional, non-entities.

Your absence makes me stronger.

I wonder if you remember that piece of *Mahabalipuram*
like I do now and forever etched into the San Bernardino sky,
pillaged and razed to the heavens above,
Here, now
Oh! Daddy
Please, please, come back for just a day.

A Pinch of Land

Why does a pinch of ancestral land
whisked in a small throw away
Absolut Vodka bottle
across 5000 miles
over 25 years ago
now buried with blessed yellow holy rice
and saffron, hibiscus flowers
and *mehendi* green leaves
from well wishers during my house warming
here in San Bernardino
here in my new backyard
mingling with the rich
native soil of yore
center the foundation
plucked from two anthems?

Eat Drink Piss Without Your Permission

Daily I pass by the bus stop ad —
"Child Abuser," emblazoned on the back
of a next-door-neighborly, hidden face.
"Trust your instincts and call," it advises.
"If only it were this easy to spot," it says
churning the bile up my adult cranium again.

Back in the day there were no 1-800-numbers,
no ads, no awareness even, but everyone knew
it happened, but didn't do squat, back then,
"Mother, I was your child, back then,
Mother," I want to say,
"I was your child too, Mother" —

Who by 9 learned to be indifferent to you
because for 3 years by then, beloved kin, "uncles"
all, everyone an "uncle", by adult sleight of hand were playing
"father figures" all around, to replace dead, young, Daddy,
all to help you, and furtively doing to me, with me,
what even the devil is not supposed to do, while you slept,
exhausted in the room next door just from raising
and tending to us.

Yes, I learned to be indifferent to you
because your love harmed more than it helped,
all the time, all the friggin' time.

And you never shut up long enough to hear us, hear me,
because we had to eat drink and piss only with
your permission, so all looked well on my skin
on the surface of things, on the face of things,
that the dermatological creams were working,
and you never shut up.

But no time to check out the underside
too burdensome, and you never shut up
'till my beloved brother almost ploughed a knife
into you, so you'd just shut up and stop calling us names
and burdens, burdens, unwanted, conceived
"as rabbits do," you said.

So we learned to hold hands together
and left you out cold, cold as you had wanted-always.

Detached attachment, your creed always, now ours.

Truly, really, even to this day, and went on to
eat drink and piss, and even be merry
without your friggin' permission
always without your friggin' permission-hah!

An Orphanage Must Be Cozier

Ungrateful seed that I am,
an orphanage must be cozier
than the styrofoam love
I got growing up
in a place called home.

Daddy died at 35,
rammed by a drunken
army truck,
no fault of his,
his dreams intact.

Mother bled on from 29,
rammed by the same drunken
army truck,
no fault of hers,
her illusions cracked.

"Uncles" of dark stripes and shades
Fondled me,
on and on from 6-12,
no fault of hers,
her bulwarks still-those deadly kin.

She ground on,
lashing out at me
with her tongue and hands,
target practice,
to still her cloying demons.

An orphanage is cozier than this,
this shambles called home.
Still,
home is love,
love is home,

continued...

and there's no two ways about that,
and no amount of therapy does erase that.

Blood is thicker than water,
and messier,
yet water slakes the thirst
better,
every time
even in a styrofoam cup.

"Ingrate, ingrate, ingrate,"
my mental tombstone
laments,
as I sit in my corner,
my thumb in my eye.
My epitaph reads
love in a styrofoam cup is home.

Rooms of Pain

Uncle—
don't go
where
no-one's
gone before.

Uncle
please
don't go
where
no-one's
gone before.

There is
no room
for kindness here
only for fumbling
and fondling
you can
but
you don't
you can
but
you won't
be the adult
and
be right.

I can't
but
I do
for I am the child
with the terrible

continued...

toxic shock
of unmet expectations.

Oh! how I ebb
and still expect
when mere
functionality
now
becomes
the feat of the day.

Cookie Crumb Clichés

They're all the same, honey, two ends,
both high functioning, they snore,
they fart, they have hidden loans,
and mothers, immutable, intractable.
Being hit by an 18 wheeler sound familiar?

They booze, they schmooze, they use,
they lose you 'coz they can't scratch your innards.

A peek at tomorrow, lines from an oxygen tank,
a catheter or two, two ends meet,
high functioning.

Untangle the tummy knots, unravel the vertebrae,
bones not yet broken, a step closer to *shantih nirvana moksha*,
call it what you will, meanwhile, Christmas comes
with its cookie-crumb clichés.

A bluff somewhere, anywhere,
with the wind lashing your face,
a sea somewhere, sucking at your soul.

The Stuff of Hands

Loving rough wise womanly hands
kneading soft the sallow dough,
pure fragrant stone ground lentils,
'till its pliable skin can be stretched
across the blinding white cheese cloth,
a nip here a tuck there till it's just right,
moon faced *papad* dough
ready to accept the oval pods
of fresh pungent black cumin seeds,
pock marking the smoothness,
red hot chilly dots burning each face
that fill this cottage industry with self taught pride —
PRIDE-*Lijjat*.

Ready now to be laid out in the tropical Indian sun,
110 degrees and more, to be dried to a crisp,
to be stored for a year, relished all over the globe
by rich and poor alike, the poor who stretch to be able
to eat vegetables and fruit, East before and now
in the tardy West, to be roasted toasted fried or nuked,
appetizer, snack, main dish, after dish crunched
over hot steaming sticky white rice
with just a drizzle of golden *ghee*,
the age old kiddies delight,
'till the taste buds burst with an Indian thirst
all across the globe.

Each crunchy bite of *Lijjat* one more hurrah for those
quiet unnamed calloused hands toiling away
under the blazing sun, reveling in the ancient
ritualistic recipe, proud forbearers of a womanly pride
and subdued glory, baked to perfection in every village,
big and small, every nook and cranny of womanly pride,
now celebrated as Gandhian pride, IMF and World Bank

style, calloused knowing hands rolling out
those doughy delights, snapping *papads*,
so that all can eat and be merry.

I Am Cschacschatti Woman

Swaying my wide wide hips to my rural mountain beat
my dark skin shining against my nappy, wiry hair coiled high
above my head as my silver hoops in my ears, in my flat,
smooth, squat nose glimmer in the dawn with thick anklets
to balance me, *Ramulamma* (often *Bangaramma*, shielding a
deadly tumor at the base of her skull,
and *Appayamma* too, blind in one eye, then the other).
I jangle my way down the verdant, moss-feathered,
iridescent mountains atop Dolphins Nose anchored
in the lazy limitless Bay of Bengal.

Planting the rhythms of my people in the raw red soil, I carry
my fresh load of pure vegetables grown with my scratches and bruises.
Squatting back on my haunches, as I turn the soft dank raw red earth
with my brass knuckle hands, our world famous, lime-green and white
striped eggplants, bright green chillies, holding Andhra infernos in
 their jackets, our plump sweet mangoes, *Banginipalli, Rassam, Romani*,
 bursting to spill their orangey yellow guts at a scratch.

I sell my load to age old clients, downhill, the city folk,
their tick-tock lives teeming with heat,
I can mock "is that a face that can afford an apple,"
and they will keep coming back for the earth's fresh groins,
famous in these parts as *yerra matti*-red earth,
kissed by the milk foamed lips of the ocean below,
its heavy mists ground into the vegetables, staining
them with lush life, staining my nails with the tell-tale henna,
gorentaku red as the earthworms comma their way
to the bright, surface, heavy and moist with the rank,
fishy odor of jumbo prawns and fish.
I am *Cschacschatti* Woman, Indira Gandhi in my own right,
made of microcredit, giving it today
out of my very own garden, my very own thatched hut,
rich with fecund cow patties, rich with chances.

My own man hoists his woven basket too
each morning in the summer,
Vizag palm, *munjellu* slithering, tumbling out their sea-shell fullness,
slender, tender green lady's fingers, deep purples in *auberjoine* glory,
the rest of the time he mopes down the mountains, the hills,
so his knees and back crackle. He has only one stop each day, the first
house that will haggle down his load for 2 red *Andhra chillies*,
smooth, curly, long, with clear translucent crimson ridges
that bite the palette, scorch the air.

There I find him, laid out in the toddy hut, cross-eyed drunk
with manhood, as the ravenous sun sets over the ozone layer.
Nothing lightens my load as rocking on my haunches, with my
hand-rolled supple cheroot in my mouth, glowing tip brightening,
smoldering my cavernous mouth, *Andhra* style, my load
for tomorrow spilling beside my prone passed out man.
I am *Cschacschatti* Woman.

Your Veluri Literary Common Kitchen Sense

Earth brown glazed over wet iridescent green
in your homespun *Venkatagiri Andhra* cotton *sari*,
Mamma, Grandmamma, Daddy's mama,
oozing wisdom and tears,
at 2 in the morning, in your stiff upright
no-nonsense British
Tudor chair reading the latest
Yeddanapoodi Sulochana Rani novel,
brimming with intrigues of family
and the heart, whose speed
reading taught me my treasured native Telugu,
the Italian of the East, reading, reading,
reading with failing nerves and eyes,
a crackling laugh, your proud literary lineage
stamped in *Veluri* genes, that keep you young
into your 80's, unlined face, sharp mind,
and Oh, that mane of hair, wavy
as the rhythmic beat of the heart,
your proud literary lineage,
shooting through your wavy, wiry hair,
and wisdom, and tears, flawed, fallen, irreverent,
never preaching, empty vessels, just
doing whatever your arthritis swollen legs
would allow through that excruciating bone-on-bone pain,
with the star shaped, scalding-white burn mark
on your right shin, no Gandhian
hypocrisy here, just plain practical common
kitchen sense, coursing down through the centuries,
'till you made your own, our own,
never flinching under the 19th century yoke
of common living, there you are, still regal
and tormented in your practical
common kitchen sense.

Aaha! That's Filter Coffee

Grandma's magic rose to meet the ceiling
and the tongues of arching mouths,
cavernous for her silky smooth filter coffee,
her nerve-numbed veteran hands picking,
roasting the home grown
beans, sun washed, sun dried.
Grinding day a legend in the land,
the bitter dust settling all over with strong
blessings from its aficionados, the craft,
an intricate tapestry of motion,
patting down the fine granules, a work of love,
into the steel filter with the family initials
emblazoned on the side, steaming water
meeting the brown rings
of heaven, only pure essence
dripping down below, poured into tiny family,
stainless steel glasses, hand milked buffalo nectar,
just a smidge added to the enveloping liquid gold,
ritually ribbon-stretched 6 yards,
cooling off just right,
to be received by eager mouths.

And in all the land, a hushed silence
for an ancient art,
then a sigh: "Aaha! That's coffee."

Dosa **Delight**

She sliced the knobbly head clean off the deep royal purple
egg plant. Pinching the moist, lively stalk between her thumb
and forefinger, she dipped the flat bottom into the gurgling sesame
seed oil, fresh stone ground that morning, warm, rich, pungent,
to rub the 400 degree cast iron *tava* skillet slick, just a smidge.

With her family ancestry molded into its pitch black, steaming
face, Great Grandma swiveled into the steamy vortex, folding
herself into the ancient creases.

The frothing bubbly lentils, hand ground, sparkled.
With a whipping circular flick of her wrist,
she poured an expert ounce or two
of the creamy contents into the inviting heat —
crackle snip, snap, shhhhhhhhh —
the crisp done *dosa* edges lifted clean off the blackened face
as she flicked chopped earth-grown, white onions glistening
in pearly oblivion, backyard green, green *Andhra chillies*,
gleaming in their scorching jackets, home grown,
somber green curry leaves, torn to unleash their virile flavor,
sprinkled in the nick of time 'till they clung to the ripening
dough, while she flipped over the browned Belgian
lace of a flaky crisp Indian delight.

Two minutes of Grandma's veteran recipe
polished off in less time than a sizzle.
Aaha, *dosa* delight!

Spiritual Sanity

My ancestral path scythes
its raggedy way on its
harsh Himalayan reality
to Mt. Sumer —
stunning, ethereal
in gauzy universal light.
Mt. Sumer —
bursting its *Kedarnath* bounds
into *Nanda*, elsewhere as *Mandakini* at *Badrinath*
crushing terrible rock,
the road, the bus, the pilgrims,
into the roaring ravine below
Ganga frothing with silty intensity
over the placid altitudinous step farms
inexorable, timeless
beckoning—
what's a few lives
for spiritual sanity.

Little Telugu Women of the Earth
(Verri Janakiamma's Voice and Spirit)

I did all that you told me to do, Mother, and it still didn't add up
to anything much. I did not have to come to America
to find that out for myself.
I did the Asian thing mother.
I did the Asian thing mother,
I shut up and did the Asian thing, shut up so hard
that it all went in deep inside and fermented into a rebellion
better dealt with in adolescence, which froths its way into
an awkward 40ish stance.
"Forget the Arts which are for the birds."
"Embrace the Sciences," you said
especially the man-heavy ones
and be a doctor or an engineer, and that's it.
That's where the future lies
That's it to life? Oh yes, or do the next best thing,
marry one so you have a sure fire future, a weighty life.
The Asian thing is but a fling into the vast vicarious parental void
that never ceases to suck up its responsibility, its obligation, its duty
blotting up any traces of visible, show-able love.

Great Grandma's published book,
"Songs of the Eccentric Heart" harks to me –
Crazy Janaki they named her after 7 little infants died in the womb
Crazy Janaki, or *eccentric Janaki* to ward off the evil eye in 1796,
so named so she could poke her thumb in the middle of the evil eye,
and live to tell her little tale, and laugh into the wind.
Great grandma Janaki in her regal purple silk *Kanchi saree*
fixing her regal stare on the streets, running down the Guntur streets
in all her wise abandon, freely flinging her very own silver coins
for anyone to pick up but mostly the city urchins, who followed
her silver pied piper trail, as free and wild eyed as her, rubbing their
dirty palms clean with *her* wealth, *better the street urchins take it*

and put it in their growling grateful bellies, she thought, *than those*
whining grasping heirs, my very own adopted darlings too,
who crave my well gotten wealth, all my own too,
that I so readily fling into the wind.

Who knew the locked stories of yore she spun while strolling
to blow off all that bloat and gas? Reciting the ancient rich,
Gayatri Mantram against the orange-stained sky,
in her gold sandals and anklets, tinkling
her very own little tune in blessed excess,
in the narrow paved, hot, Guntur streets,
where no little *Telugu* women ventured,
married to their precious pots and pans, in the kitchen,
too cocooned to hear her rough tongue struggle
for two hours daily to learn from *dorasani* (Madam) Lucy *ingilipeesu*,
or *English*, as they called it, while seated in *her country*,
and her paying Lucy with her very own gold,
so she could master all that funny grammar, and so few rich words,
so she could use the same words over and over,
to say different things into the wind, no shades,
no volume in this new tongue, but useful to tell her own *harikatha*
one day in the lyrical Italian of the East,
the *firangees* (foreigners) called her lovely *Telugu* right to her face,
ensuring that she would sing her own tune one day at the feet of her
mother, wounded with the lost blood of all those lost babies,
sagging her womb to the ground, the most beautiful sight there is—
Oh Curdled Mother, conjoined parent-both mother and father,
all the time *notgoodenough* for anyone, anytime-you and I both.
I cannot walk so I dance in these hot, narrow Guntur streets,
because I have so much song in my heart, so I bought the whole
street, and named it after you, and each evening I spin a new language
with tuneful words to sing out loud and proud, accompanied
by new music from the tiny bells of my gold anklets,
tied to my tiny feet, our age-old anthem, which your mother felt
before you, and then you, now me, with this wild song in my heart,
a wild beat in my step, singing into the wind, to all the little *Telugu*

continued...

women who can hear my very own *Harikatha*, on my very own
street, and here it is and now it is yours too.

Mothers of the earth do not create the non-home
where your daughters, your little women, have to unlearn all
that you learned, and passed on with your special recipe of bile,
that children can be burdens, who only need to ace all tests
they dare bring home in order to be fed, clothed, and housed,
making love an economic bond, where "no" is the heartfelt motto
meaning, "go away" 'till the little women go deep inside,
and the easily swayed, choose, and live your life, for endless days
to come, pleasing your every strong whim, and the less breakable
you twist into break-away, knotted, salted pretzels of independent
achievement, whose later pleasure you cannot even taste
vicariously, having thrown them to the winds of vagrant chance.
They will not need you if you choose not to be needed.
Your heart says you can, your head says you can't, and in your heart,
you say you can, in your head, you say you can't, so you give life
a head and you lose all your heart and unmake all their sunshine.

Spare them the Asian euphemism, worse than no visible love at all,
 "As long as you are happy, I am," when the truth is that their success
does not meet your measure, daughters, little women of the earth,
when all it is about is fucking the "right" man, if you're astrologically
lucky for making little clones of him and his revered mother, already
married, till death do them part, in heaven, that no bond on earth
can put asunder, a contract in hell, for the little women,
blood, gore and guts, more, blood, gore and guts, no matter
what you do, a crapshoot before you die.

Why try if you're going to die, daughters, little women
of the earth, try, try and try again, because you are going to die,
care giving is an alternate universe, dead to sleep,
you never finish first, lucky if you're dead last, faultless.

Mothers of the earth, do not make non-homes
where your little women have to unlearn all that you have learned
and passed down with your special recipe of bile.

No no no — not at all
making a home must be fun not a chore.
Molding practical women and theoretical men tilts the floor.
Making suffering look easy is no virtue, but a sure prescription
for a frozen back, then butt, adhesion, tendon, then brain, a shoulder
or two, in ortho PT speak, whereby no-one gains.
Such high tolerance for preventable pain is no badge of courage,
wherein your old wounds transfer into projected misery,
for our fragile, growing daughters, our little women,
maternal transference is projectile
vomiting, acidly burning as it flies, and stains
No no, not at all —

So much professional narcissism, wherein climbing the ladder,
while chasing your own tail, spells early emotional rigor mortis,
a good shield you think, making suffering look easy is no virtue at all,
and pretending not to care is detached attachment,
so much superficiality is poison in any nest.
Show your little women that even crows kiss beautifully,
that the grass is blue and the sky is green,
so that they don't flee you with glee, defining love by negation,
opening doors porous to predator priests,
incestuous uncles.

Mothers of the earth do not make non-homes
where your daughters, our little women, have to unlearn
all that you have learned,
and passed down with your special recipe of bile.
Little women of the earth, flex your spines to fly
into your earthbound nests.

continued...

The hardest truth you will challenge is you, yourself,
and them, your family-spouses, husbands, their families,
your other family-mothers, siblings, and their families,
your community, your state.
Truth in concentric circles is to face suffering beyond your ken
on their terms when knowing your own truth, your reality
of what makes sense dissolves old bonds that were broken anyway,
to forge new ones for a new day, palliative care of the heart
starts at home, when all there is to unlearn, and learn,
is to know the ancient Vedic truth:
bless us with the knowledge of what is spiritual.
Bless us with the knowledge of what is material.
Bless us with the intelligence to know the difference,
and wisdom to combine the best of both.

Little women of the earth, daughters,
truth is all there is,
so you can be alone and alive.

(Prayer to Lord Vinayaka quoted from *The Holy Book of Neo-Vedic Prayers: Prayers of Power and Inspiration* by Shri Sampath Bhoopalam, 2nd ed; N.Y., N.Y: Himalaya Publishing House, 1990:1.

"Injoy"

(Inspired by and dedicated to Bangaramma)

Train whistle tearing the pallid still air of that hot summer
so long ago,   *Ooooooeeeeeeee Aieeeeeeeeeeee*,
shredding the unmoving village calm at its tracks
to midnight bits, *Dhak dhak dhak dhak*, the dust, ash
and black coal streaking my young grey hair to its roots,
my yet unlined face with a throbbing brown wart,
pinched uncertainly under the steel rims of my glasses.
Speeding into the long night while I, numbed in the corner,
clutching my money pouch wrapped around my waist
barely bulging under my *saree*, clutching those twelve
displaced tiny hands, fleeing with the tumors of life
at the base of my skull to the city, far, far away
from the squalor left behind.
"Injoy"
gather your belongings
start a fresh.
so I told my grandchild.

If you think they will cheat they will. He did, all newly returned
from England, barrister and all his newly minted wisdom between
the black leather bound books, underlined with his black pen, rural
wife that he left behind, too earth bound, too naïve, too illiterate.
So he chased skirt and then some more 'till he bled the family
fortune, and lands to her, and her, and her.
Don't be "*intiki jushta, porugki sri malaxmi*"
a curse at home, a blessing abroad.
"Injoy,"
gather your belongings,
start afresh.
So I told my grandchild.

continued...

If you think they will drink , they will. He did 'till his eyes
were crimson with loss and bourbon shaded with Marlboro swirls,
tinged with bellowing pity, 'till the deafening silence of desertion
turned to rage, lashing out at the boys with belt buckles sobered up
with blood, 'till he smashed his conniving widowed aunt's bald head
against the ancestral family well.
"Injoy,"
gather your belongings
start afresh.
So I told my grandchild.

If you think it will get worse, it will. Shock the brain,
shock his reality, the city psychiatrist warned,
so we did for years, and years of his solitary seclusion,
with a box of Marlboros for company each week.
When the Marlboro man comes a-calling, and he will,
when the smoke chokes his lungs, and even the bag tied to his throat,
or the wires trailing him down won't hide the bloody sputum,
the painful phlegm, 'till his lungs and throat sagged with cancer, the
medical bag lines trailing his past.
So dye your hair, even if your teeth stand out.
"Injoy,"
gather your belongings
start afresh.
So I told my grandchild.

And before the hideous rattling comes
Drrrrr drrrrrrr drrrrrr drrrrr DRRRRRR
at the end of an undignified terrifying, sapped throat,
and it will, gather the family around in the garden,
on rattan lawn chairs and take the photo of your life,
even if he doesn't want you in it, even if the stripes of hurt
and pain poke out, gather them around, the tiny tots,
the rasping elders, and everyone in between still left

standing, crying huge, unseen jagged sobs.
Nibble a ripe *rasam*, the best mango around, 'till the yellow juice
of its life dribbles down your elbows.
"Injoy,"
gather your belongings
start afresh.
So I told my grandchild.

Then after, hold the best memorial with family from all across
the country to respect and dignify his memory. You must.
Then later —much, much later —gulp down life, go in the backyard,
reach for the *shikakai*, caress your hair with its fragrant lather,
pamper your skin with *Mysore* sandalwood soap,
whose buttery creamy suds will stretch your skin,
massage your scalp with swirly *sambrani* mists
'till your whole body goes limp with joyful relief.
"Injoy,"
gather your belongings
start afresh.
So I told my grandchild.

If you think the kids will cry, they will. Conjoined parent—
both mother and father all the time, *notgoodenough* for anyone,
anytime. Raise them right, teach them love and gladness,
show them the sky and grass, make them humble to chance,
to respect him —they need to.
Compromise crumbles through each crack, sacrifice sticks to the
bones, not letting go even when shaken, dusted.
Wake up quietly, even if it's 4:30 a.m., slip into the bath
to rip open the crackling tissue paper that cocoons that gem,
that oval savior, the imported joy of the translucent *Pears*,
lock yourself in its lather this time, pamper your gristly follicles
with Sun-silk, take all day if you want, if you have to,
then step out anew with your smooth pliant skin.
So go shopping, make independent choices between a dress

continued...

or a bauble, bubble gum or candy with sweet relief.
"Injoy,"
gather your belongings
start afresh.
So I told my grandchild.

If you think the best will come, it will. Crack open the hard nuts
of your favorite walnuts mixed in with the plumpest raisins.
Let the ridged nutty cranial flavor whisk you away.
Suffer when young and your spine will take it,
suffer when old and your heart will die and crack wide open.
So turn on the radio to the hardest beat, and
swing your feet off the ground, rope in a friend or two,
pick the voluntary, not the obligatory.
Reach for the sky, you might grab a star, reach for the earth
and all you might get is dirt.
If you go looking for smooth pebbles, be ready
to get misshapen rocks.
If you go looking for limes make margaritas.

"Injoy"	"Injoy"
Gather your belongings	Gather your belongings
start afresh.	start afresh
So I told my grandchild.	So I told my grandchild.

So I told my grandchild.

Svabhimaanam

(Self Realization)

Boo hoo
Boo hooo
Boo hoooo
Boo who.

Yoo hoo
You hooo
You hoooo.

You who.

So *Ammamma* (Mom's mom) said
Quite under her brea(d)th.

The Man In the Moon

> Chandamama raave zhabilli raave
> Kondekki raave gogi poolu thaave
> *Chandamama raave zhabilli raave.*
> ~Ancient *Telugu* lullaby.

See my small frail pathetic spouse in the moonlight, one eyed now,
and bent over with my care, bending over my 5 little ones sprung
from my doped and glazed loins, my alcohol clogged liver and veins,
my yellowed nicotine breath, from my stale life, from my red-lit
cigarettes ground into her pale skin, all burnt and fried
into jagged rings in front of those little scared eyes,
'till it rendered my oldest boy mute, and strangled
within himself, 'till it robbed the marrow out of the second one
in his wheelchair fading away from muscular dystrophy,
'till it delivered the 2 little girls into sodden marriages of their own,
all black and blue, 'till the tiniest one fled with her husband
to start over in a sane peace, in a land of milk and honey,
far West from me in the United States, of course.

And now, here I lie in my open cage, in and out of the hospital,
wondering if I mocked the Man in the Moon once too often,
imprisoned in my blurry blaze of irrational screams and taunts,
which broke my aged widowed mother's heart and bank,
of peeing and pooping all over my spouse's parents' carpets
to beat them into my ground 'till they could not
raise their heads in their own backyard.

If I mocked the Man in the Moon once too often then,
he mocks me now, inside my tight lungs, my cross-eyed heart,
my pocked liver, my dead fingers, my spent life,
the only one I got a chance to live here.

Man in the Moon, shine your soft light with mercy on us,

scratch up over the mountain, and bring us those blossoms,
Man in the Moon, shine your mercy on me now,
or what else is left, but to light up and go.

Oh Look, Tsunami Tsunami

1896 I think no birth records yet, but around that time
I was born in Guntur, Andhra Pradesh, *Jagadeeswari*,
they called me to survive the Tsunami of 1906,
which came unseen unheard and knocked me
to the top of the roof where I sat for eleven days
orphaned, clinging to the red tiles with the skin
of my bowels, so much rude diarrhea, wondering
if they related to my brown face enough to come
and get me, no food, no water, no clothes,
just ashen bodies floating by, and all the crap from me,
from every body dear God, I thought, so much crap
I could not breathe.

I told myself that day there is no life, just crap, so grab it
and make it your own, I said to myself,
and grabbed a little orphan girl
who became my very own in all that stench,
Tsunami, I called her and told her too,
"Oh look, Tsunami, Tsunami, there is no life
just crap so grab it and make it your own
'till your eyes fill with tears."

Four years later I was married and he was tall and strong
and very, very dark, taller than the Tsunami wave, I thought,
and we became a sweet little family
in spite of all that stench.

"Dilli Durbar"

    My Poem
        SS# 555-555-555.

Welcum to the Dilli Durbar
it's how to say it-Dilli
Mum, Sir, vhere you like to sit?
What you like to eat? Naan, Paratha, Tandoor Tikka
Yes Mum, Yes Sir.

You think it Indian desi, but it Moghlai Persian-heehee.
To you all the same.
I lickie lickie your boots
not cuz
you tipie tipie big
which I no ever see
cuz you see the biggie biggie sahib there
he own all this
and so he take
all your biggie biggie tips
so he pay my airfare here
my food, my ratty room and stinky bathroom
so he say.
I say I his for life.

No I lickie lickie you
cuz you not know what you see
right in front of you
I be Mehican or Afghani or desi
or what you like me to be
but you give me one chance to be whatever I wanna be
the desi there
sitting at table near you
he think I shit
so I show him
how you say

                                          continued...

*the finger in my clever mind
only of my unclean hand
heeheehee.
What he know about me yaar.*

*I no doctor
but I civil enjenaer
in Jhumrithalayya
I Big Shot
big bangla big gadi
with Rana blood
inside me honorable
where it matter most
i pure white
you burger eating brown arsed slow foul blooded desi
Hum Kaale hain to kya hua dilwale hain
my chumdi/hide oily brown
like your chicken koorma you licking
my dil pure white
so what you know about me yaar.*

*You desi and just like my sahib
I his Beverrly bangla no want
I his murrrsedeez no want
I his dollarrs no want
only he my brother by blood
from my grandmother Nani
he mix greed in blood
which stick to his body
also to the bottom of his soul
which take him down quick
to the bottom of the Gunga
when his time come.*

*He know he know too
so I spit on his greedy groin*

so how you say
till it stick where the sun don't shine
and go up his brown bad arse
cuz he and the desi jus like me
old chewed gum
stuck
i no go home
i no stay here
where i go?

Yes mum, Yes sir.
Pleej cum agin, pleej cum agin
To this Dilli Durbar.

H1 Bliss: Let it Be

Colonial clones
in their Benz's their BMW's
Volkswagens
with nary a cross word
or disagreement
outwards
Commonwealth British trained
thoroughly styled
"Yes sir. No sir.
Yes Massa. No Massa.
Whatever you say Sir.
Left right, left right."
Round pegs in round holes
shaved to fit the work milieu
bureaucratic and all
whatever however
perrrrfect work ethic
perrrrfect etiquette
perrrrfect moneymakers
perrrrfect capital captains.
stunted caterpillars.

Inside
seething cauldrons
of Gandhian rebellion
civil and cured
in the face of
Lou Dobbsian apoplectic ire
Dr. James Dobsonian religious rage
round pegs in square holes
rules restrictions
applications forms, forms, forms
go here go there

do this do that
not that not this
corporate courtesy.

Taxation without representation.
Still-even *now*.
Fate.
Let it be.

Fate.
Let it be.
$ bliss on the wings of a plane
carrying them out of
the political squalor of chances,
never given never taken,
frozen talents in small pools of unending thirst,
cram schooling their way out of patchwork poverty.
Even if the head is severed from the body of growth
go there where the $ is King.

Who needs that
Scylla and Charybdis
all over again, and again, and again
the $ falls
and *we all fall down*
ring around the rosie
just stay in Boise.
It's a brave new world
where the $ is common currency
where the $ is the common tongue.
Viva H1 bliss.

Colonial Sell Out

I write necessarily with a post colonial, forked tongue
as the greats before me, Kamala Markandeya, and the other
irreverent *Kamala* before her, R.K. Narayan, Palagummi
Padmaraju, V.S. Naipaul, Derek Walcott.

Harivamshrai Bachchan actually unfettered, unleashed free verse
to its great heights. The commonwealth crap tried hard to rub out,
snuff out my scuffed tongue. But what is all mine, and still is,
is that I am part Dravidian, part Aryan, Hitlerized in the dumb
Colonial Occident, as pure hate. Fuck that bastard for stealing
my ancestry. For what is all mine, still is, is my reverent scarlet
temple *swasthika*, so Indian, so very Indian.

My native roots, deep in the bowels of the Dravidian South,
my Visakhapatnam, my Chennai, my Pune, my Mumbai,
Anglicized to Vizag, Madras, Poona, Bombay.
Fuck the British.

I am NOT converted in my own land —
a colonial sellout.

Physician Heal Thyself

I am a proud *Dravida* from *Periar, Papanasanam*,
South India, God dammit.
The original thing, even in India, before you Aryan hordesmen
branded and *casted* me, a proud *Dravida* all of 5 ft. 6 in.,
bronze and sculpted, who pulled myself up by my Brahmin
boot straps to make it here, in our Americas,
as a micro specialized physician in the Southland.

When the glare hits the tinted windows of my S-Series BMW,
I am totally in the dark about what's outside.
I put on my special ordered special tinted Ray Bans
that no one else can get, by the way,
special ordered, special made for a special *Dravida* man.

I'm pure inside and out, and no mongrel, proud
of where I'm from. So listen up you melting pot mongrels,
I'm not from *Negrito*, Moorish, Slavic, Mongol, Aryan,
Persian blood, though you want me to teach my children so.
No Hindu, Muslim, Christian, Parsi, Zoroastrian, Bahaiin, Buddist
will undermine my true roots. I am a true *Dravida*
I am a true *Dravida*.

"Canyugis"

In India caste was all the rage.
no-one rested till they knew
which one I was —
Brahmin, Kamma, Reddy, Naidu.

Fed up, I moved
to the land of milk and honey,
of streets paved with gold,
pie-in-the-sky U.S.

Here, doctors, dentists,
students, neighbors,
postal carriers,
grocery passersby exclaim,
"Love the accent, soooo British",
"I love yours too."
"Love the tan."
"Not a tan, just melanin."
Then inquire,
still
"Where are you from?"
"From here," I deadpan,
no salve for fascist curiosity.

"Where are you from?"
They ask over and over
so I retort, "Can you guess?"
"*Canyugis*, you say?
Where is that,
an island somewhere?"
"Yes, yes", I say,
"a beautiful island in a borderless world,

all global and interlocked
in an infinite web of humanity
on one planet earth."

But the pigeon-holing thirst
has yet to be slaked
boxed, stamped, and duly branded,
and so "*Canyugis*" it is!

www.opportunity.ca.us

It's just 7 miles of neck connecting the strung San Bernardino body
to the withering LA head through the 210. That was just 2 years ago
as the rapidly stretching 210 lopped off the orange heads of the groves
throbbing its way into Fontana, Rialto, Redlands, and Highlands
for the sprouting orange mission tiles of cul-de-sac sub prime dreams
nestling along its torso, the new golden pioneers
of the dust bowl west. The San Andreas fault cuts below it all
tectonic, pulsating as the earth shivers, shivers, shakes,
shivers and shakes all the time,
3.7, 4.2, 5.7 —
Whoa.

The train tracks slice through the 3rd Street sprawl of grueling grime,
of carouseled muck and crime, pan handling pokes its bony fingers
along the spine of the 215, expanding, retracting, constructing,
concreting, turning the earth over, and over, tax payer dollars
whirling in the Orange show curse of wet things to come,
MAPEI, Walmart, Home Depot, Mervyns, new and old,
here one minute, closed the next,
Riverside particulates grinding in bagpipe lungs.

I-10, the 210, the 215 meet, cross over to squeeze triangular growth
from this shaky ground, freeways to access, to opportunity.

210 W, 8/11/08, 12:10 p.m. slow lane shut off with 20 linear
Matich monsters from Del Rosa to Waterman, a legal construction
cone spins surreally across 4 lanes, backed by an illegal, careening
Honda Civic 360 degreeing in tow, smashes, bangs into a legal Toyota
Corolla slamming brakes in the fast lane, to whirl onto the pavement,
air bags fully deployed, hood mawkishly open, gun metal grey
smoke pouring all over the still, watching traffic, illegal fiddling
with the radio ipod maybe, txt msging, or dvd scrolling while the limp
air bag gets stuffed back into the black gaping hole.

The 210's neck bristles with illegal street racing
Vrrrrrrrrrrrrrrrrrrrrroooooooom
pumping up the volume here in "LA's lil ghetto"
its growth canker, while in dying LA, a 77-year-old woman,
waiting, celebrates her birthday wish,
clutching a gritty rosary of prayer, of hope.

The Eye Of the Storm

Raw red angry concentric spreading wrath on Ch. 2 of New Orleans.
I am in a seedy motel, off, off the Bourbon maze where the lice
itch to crawl all over the semen-seeded side of a smelly, smelly town
where a honeymoon unraveled.
EVACUATE!

Earlier, gumbo at Cuckoos, Chicory rancid coffee on a jazzed-up
sidewalk, the cracks swallowing any pride left over.

We join the miles and miles of a ribboning stretch beside
the somnolent Bayou aflame with the bubbly eyes atop floating gators.

After 38 hours of highway jams, furtive wayside restroom stops
all I got was a thrombotic leg and heart, hidden inside a flailing
marriage.

And So Spot Said To Fido

Pigsy had just barely died, and so brown Spot said to black Fido,
newly born, "Stick to the land you dope, where the curly, frilly
American flag flies proud with the square chewed-up one
in the middle fluttering loud on the splotched aluminum fence
on this triangular-tipped homestead with the bulging semen-stained
chaise lounges sunning themselves beside the teabag-heavy orange
groves drizzled by bees, sniped at by the thick nectar coating,
the red rusty tractor on this condo-pocked neighborhood
where all goes up, then down, then up again, then down, down,
down again, where our tail-pulling mouth-grabbing kids slide down
their yellow, red, plastic play toys, and be, ho hum, Fido."

"And so," Spot said to Fido, as he suckled under her
"you 'lil thing, still growing, don't go being
Ferdinand Magellan, Bartholomew Diaz.
Around here wanderlust kills
just as surely as grandma's gout."
"Woof, woof," beamed Fido.

The jet-black dub Hummer with its hunting lights galore
lumbered up the slope wheezing, panting, coughing
braking violently at the stop sign, then rolled down hill
over a blinking Fido smack dab in the middle of the street,
12" tall, thin as a rail, "yip, yip."

Much later, Matt from his lone humble farm, across the street,
scraped Fido off the sidewalk into a shoebox,
rang his neighbor's doorbell,
and with all due respect graciously delivered the mutt
to be buried.

And So the Stupid Critic Said

And so the stupid critic said in 2003
Cerebral...intellectual to the point of stupidity.

And so the wise publisher/poet said in 2008
Powerful work with an emotional punch
Healing spiritual wisdom.

Go figure.

Later duly chided,
"*Poetry?* Write a novel."

So just write
and write some more
furiously fast
'till the poetic words
ooze out your pores
'till the carpal tunnel crushes your phalanges
'till your right hip dislocates
'till 2 a.m. 3 a.m.
'till your batteries drain
'till the marrow in your bones
sucks its way into your words
because the words wrench your guts
because you have to
'till the words lick the light of day.

And so Mother Theresa would have said,
write anyway!

Hung Out On a Shingle

A primeval circle drags on
where the life of imagination counts
for very little, if at all.
Very real symptoms first pluck at the brow,
then sear it, burning holes in the forehead, the scalp,
stinging, writhing, leaping, crackling like a
live viral wire in the brain, contorting vision,
sapping energy, draining sight through a bulging eye.

That's what it took before the shingle masters,
the doctors, took seriously, *two weeks later,*
a virulent form of the *shingles indeed.*
Extensive dental surgery *may lead to this,*
or any chronic stress, any suppressed immune system,
the causes still very unclear in a technologically
advanced, advancing hurried system, botched care,
with the dentist defensive, the primary care awol,
all it took was a vigilant pharmacist to see it,
an *attentive vigilant* medical sibling to follow through each day,
and then, only in the urgent care at 9 p.m., promptly,
with the nurse rolling her eyes to this indifference,
did the alert doctor make the *obvious* diagnosis,
no dangerous denials here, as the trigeminal nerve
is a dangerous contender for attention.

Speedy prescriptions dispatched,
the all night, all day pharmacy unable to read
the illegible Rx, filling only half the note,
the thread bare pharmacist shaking his head
in disbelief, a call from them the next day
to the urgent care to fix things, in the meanwhile
filling the prescription twice, in error,
but these things take time, slow burning time, till the patient

continued...

tossing and turning in bed rest (*hah!*) finally picks up the phone,
ragged after 2 hours on it locating the still awol doctor,
her irritated nurse kicking it back to urgent care,
then kicking it to an optometrist,
holy cow, because the eye may go?,
with the dentist intoning "it's all in your imagination",
not his doing in the first place, just *maybe*,
dangerous denials leading to a year's worth
of neuralgic twitches and shocks it took
the steady calm involved physicians to undo,
till the circle of futility catches up
with the spasmodic crushing pain,
perfect prescription for invisibility
to scream *arrrrrrrrrrrrrrrrrrrgh*.

The patient admits she's an HMO,
chocolate-colored, 50 something-year-old,
perfect prescription for invisibility in an alchemist
world of complex procedures, textbook infections,
live viruses getting us all the time
as we fight to fend them off,
one nerve left, that's it.
Perfect prescription for invisibility.

When did all this happen so fast
where patients need to cower behind
blue shields of valor, of scouring for *good* care,
for respect for life, for dignity of care?

Perfect prescriptions for invisibility,
profiles in typical care today,
so much for life, liberty, and happiness,
so much for the Hippocratic Oath,
so much for not doing harm, above all,
so much for the good ones, so few and far

and in between the indifferent,
so much for patient care today
in a bruised bright brave new world,
so much for hanging out a shingle today
in a cramped competing insular alchemist world,
so much for hanging out a shingle today,
so much for the shingles.

Change

In a surreal 1929 like ethereality,
a $170 million Inaugural celebration
with the American flag duly pinned
onto a reluctant lapel,
in a John Woo, Swarovski crystal ball gown,
starts with the seeds of hope and change
in a blistering cold swearing in ceremony
of community giving-and-sharing,
with the Bushiites still at the helm at NSA,
and the Clintonites brought back
and secure in every other post,
with the Supreme Court Justice flubbing the oath
so it has to be repeated away from prying eyes,
to be legal, only this time with no bible.
2009.

While the small donors who gave and gave,
and then gave some more, in tiny increments,
away from prying eyes, $$ they had too few of,
while the $ 800 billion bail out still swings above their heads,
a Damocles sword of hope, of change, wish they could
clutch tightly onto their scarce $$ a little while longer,
to their hope a little while longer,
change comes alright, huh?, "Yes, it did",
"Yes, we can", "yes, we did, and we will."
We have to.

My Mumbai Oh My Mumbai

9:45 p.m., 10:30 p.m. 11/25/08,
boom boom boom ratatatatat
my Mumbai oh my Mumbai bombed into a burning shell
my Mumbai, place of my birth,
my mother's womb, my daddy's loins,
my blood, my soil,
my Mumbai of fashionable esplanades,
of Marine Drive and Colaba Causeway,
of valiant Shivaji who got the British so sneakily,
of grinding dust mixed in with dirt poor sweat and toil,
Daddy in his dashing military uniform, shiny buttons,
polished boots, Asoka epaulets, with his starry-eyed wife
on his arm, me kicking holy hell in her proud swollen belly,
a solid gold tennis bracelet bursting with India's finest pearls
xoxoxoxoxoxoxoxoxoxoxoxoxoxoxoxoxox
to mark this small occasion of life, the promise of it,
my Mumbai, theirs, ours of carefree movie going, of "Bollywood",
popcorn dreams, starry nights, better days to come
surely, a death defying, youthful hope and joy.

And then this.
Boom boom boom boom again and *boom boom boom.*
A new kind of attack in poisoned dinghies shooting through
this age old Gateway making common commuter targets of all,
60 hours of never ending gouging terror,
streaming sterile into my cocooned U.S. home,
internet, tv, sinotic blue, streaming video isolating us
from the bleeding pain and gore over there.
Yet a visceral, live, leaping, viral ache writhes in my hurting head,
connecting me in a straight bloodline to those dead,
grievously injured.
Just a 25-year-old, there on American corporate business,
his lively fiancée awaiting their wedding the next week
simply too good for the barrel of an AK 47
snouted into his face in Café Leopold

continued...

by one much younger than him in a "normal T-shirt."
And here old Larry King asks incredulously
why Bombay is now called Mumbai-when did this happen?

Let's send in our better-trained FBI negotiating teams
to help those brown locals down there
messing up a perfectly good Thanksgiving turkey here,
with a Black Friday trampling to death of a Wal Mart boy
over a frenzied 20% off on an HDtv
Death comes in very many forms, sanity in very few.
The only world leaders stepping up coming from
Britain, Australia, and Israel while we chew on events for 48 hours
hanging back to "monitor the situation as it unfolds"
(till we realize none is safe or immune)
counting the American casualties,
Mumbai and Mumbaiites only good as a cesspool of lowly
outsourcing for our insatiable western appetites,
Thanksgiving or no thanks giving.

When the smoke of hate clears,
and the grateful survivors never stop thanking
the brave kind Indian army and navy commandos,
and the charred dust of violence never settles,
for the "face of evil does not necessarily look evil"
as an American survivor found out,
teenage-or-thereabouts-terrorists
holding two nuclear tipped countries
and a terror weary world aghast,
where a swinging army commando
helicoptered down into the jewish house
hits home when an orphaned 2 year old face
cries and stings the conscience,
no collateral damage here.
Where Asoka and Gandhi have been tried and tried
maybe it's time to give Kasturba a shot.

No one knows—
who/why/when, the 24/7 news cycle spits out, over and over,
as an inarticulate, distraught, local man wrests the microphone
from the frustrated CNN Sarah Sider.
Here, real at last, in all our faces but only for a second:
"Let us speak, let us speak, so the whole world knows."
This hydra-headed virus now connects us all in one simple,
tragic, bloody, brotherhood.
No-one one knows, but only that it comes,
that it does not stop dragging its bloody imprints across
the Gandhian *khaddar*, outlines of peace and non violence
shredded to bits in the Taj, the Oberoi, the Chabad House,
Café Leopold, Shivaji Chatrapati Railway station, Casa Women's
and Children's Hospital, what's next, a grenade into heaven?
Rabbis, Lopez's, Anoushka's, Smiths, Joe's, and God
twisted and tossed into the charred mayhem —
My Mumbai, oh my sweet, sweet Mumbai —
primeval belly shock, bone shock.
We shudder with you over the violence of ignorance.
ARRRRRRRRRRRRRRRRRRRRRRRRRRRGH.

The blathering talking heads speculate,
"Was it the *Deccan Mujahideen?*"
while packing in bite-sized history lessons on India
with no time for analysis, for reflection over rampant, ignorant
speculation, 24/7 is a long time to fill, bloody feuding even
longer still.
NO-ONE KNOWS ANYMORE
So shut the fuck up will ya and read
Dennis Leary's *Why We Suck: A Feel Good
Guide to Staying Fat, Loud, Lazy and Stupid.*
Maybe only he knows.
Ask him.

About the Author

Sheela Sitaram Free ("Doc Free") was born in Mumbai, India and has spent equal halves of her life in India and in America. Her B.A. is in English Literature and Language, her M.A. is in English and American Literature and Language. She also has a M.A. in Hindi and a Ph.D. in the Contemporary American Novel. For twenty-two years she has taught all across the United States in universities, colleges, and community colleges revealing her lifelong passion for the power of words, especially in the context of World Literature. Her motto has always been *quality education for quality students who can least afford it*. She has received national awards for excellence in innovative teaching. Having triumphed over traumas in her life by spotting kindness, compassion, and grace in all that she sees whether it be the Himalayan highs or the lows of her daughter's death, she etches her poetry with the passionate rhythms of joyful pain. They are written with a necessarily forked-tongue, with a post-colonial vision and includes poems celebrating San Bernardino, triumphing during and after unbearable loss, separation, and pain, capturing great grandmothers and their ancestral wisdom, and evoking post-colonial images.

She is an adventurer at heart, a globe trotter like her late father Major V.S. Sitaram, and her quadrilingual background allows her to explore a rich tapestry of experience. She inherits a rich literary tradition from her paternal grandmother, Alemelu's, side — the famous *Panchatantra* fables, and Andhra's *harikatha and burrakatha* genres whose oral narratives weave literary landscapes to this day under village *banyan* trees. Her earliest inspirations were both her grandmothers whose stories painted magical portraits she could not wait to soak up each day, and the passion for verse of her school teachers, and university professors. She is committed to performance poetry in modern rhythms enlivened by the ancient folksy lilt of narrative poetry. She has zigzagged her way to happiness that she finds in serendipitous encounters at home and around the globe where she combines work, volunteerism, and play to mold rich experiences at every corner while being deeply committed to the education of the disadvantaged all over the world.

She now lives and teaches in California.

www.ingramcontent.com/pod-product-compliance
Lightning Source LLC
Chambersburg PA
CBHW051450290426
44109CB00016B/1702